THE SUMMER BEFORE SIXTH GRADE WORKBOOK

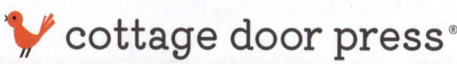

Student Notes

- Try to find a quiet place to work away from distractions and, as much as possible, try to enjoy these activities.

- Remember, you are learning new concepts that may be tricky to grasp at first, and need practice. It's OK to ask for help!

- You do not need to complete each page in one session. Always stop before you grow tired, and come back to the same page another time.

- The answers to the activities are on pages 123–128.

Copyright © 2025 Cottage Door Press, LLC
5005 Newport Drive, Rolling Meadows, Illinois 60008
www.cottagedoorpress.com

Written by Nina Filipek and Michael J. Ward
Cover art by Helen Prole
Illustrated by Simon Abbott, Mattia Cerato, Genie Espinosa, Adam Linley, and Helen Prole
Additional images used under license from Shutterstock.com
Educational Consultant: Maria Luce

All rights reserved. No part of this publication may be reproduced, stored in a retrieval system, or transmitted, in any form or by any means, electronic, mechanical, photocopying, recording, or otherwise, without the prior permission of the copyright holder.

ISBN: 979-8-89019-075-8

Gold Stars™ is a trademark of Cottage Door Press, LLC.
Cottage Door Press® and the Cottage Door Press® logo are registered trademarks of Cottage Door Press, LLC.

Contents

Language Arts and Reading	4
Writing	36
Decimals and Fractions	62
Measurement, Data, and Geometry	94
Answers	123

Language Arts and Reading

Student Notes

The activities in this section will help you learn how to:

- Extend your vocabulary and read texts for purpose, understanding, and enjoyment.

- Practice the use of standard English grammar including prepositions, adverbs, conjunctions, and punctuation.

- Explore a variety of fiction and nonfiction texts, including Native American myths, poetry, science, and history.

You may choose to work on the activities independently, or you may want help from a parent or other adult at the start of an activity.

Contents

Prepositions	6	Responding to Treasure Island	18
Perfect Tenses	7	Raven Steals the Light	20
Conjunctive Adverbs	8	Responding to Raven Steals the Light	22
Correlative Conjunctions	9	Remarkable Eyes	24
Commas in Lists and Clauses	10	Comparing Information	26
Commas After Tag Questions	11	Louis Braille Biography	28
Fragments and Run-On Sentences	12	Comparing Different Texts	30
Connotative Language	14	Jabberwocky	32
Formal and Informal Language	15	Making a Claim	34
Treasure Island	16	Answers	123

Prepositions

A **preposition** is a connecting word. Prepositions usually answer the questions **where** or **when**, and are followed by the objects (nouns) they are referring to.

After school I am going **to** the gym.   We put bread **in** the shopping basket.
The boy was sitting **beside** his dog.   Sakib walked **down** the busy street.

Choose a preposition from the box to complete each sentence.

opposite   between   to the left   to the right   beside

The ball went ....*to the left*.... of the goal posts.

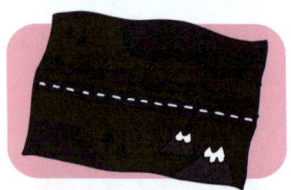
The highway is ....*beside*.... the river.

The restaurant was on the ....*opposite*.... side of the road.

There was a fence ....*between*.... the two houses.

"If we go ....*to the right*.... we should arrive at the beach."

Note for student: This activity provides practice in using directional prepositions to complete sentences.

Perfect Tenses

Perfect tense is used to describe an action that is already completed or done by a certain point of time in the past or the future.

past perfect
I had read the book.
We had visited Canada.
They had walked home.

present perfect
I have read the book.
We have visited Canada.
They have walked home.

future perfect
I will have read the book.
We will have visited Canada.
They will have walked home.

Write the perfect **past**, **present**, and **future** tenses of these verbs.

	past perfect	present perfect	future perfect
eat	had eaten	have eaten	will have eaten
dance	had danced	have danced	will have danced
drive	had driven	have driven	will have driven
clean	had cleaned	have cleaned	will have cleaned
play	had played	have played	will have played
sleep	had slept	have slept	will have slept
swim	had swum	have swum	will have swum
sing	had sang	have sang	will have sang

Note for student: The perfect tense is formed by using the present/past/future form of the verb 'to have' and the past participle of the main verb (walked, drank, built, etc.).

Conjunctive Adverbs

A **conjunctive adverb** is used to provide a link to a previous thought or sentence, and introduce a new thought or sentence. Here are some examples.

in addition	moreover	→ to make an additional point
however	nevertheless	→ to provide a contrasting thought
for instance	for example	→ to give clarification on a point
therefore	consequently	→ to draw a conclusion based on a previous point

Read the following letter. Choose appropriate **conjunctive adverbs** to complete the sentences. Some may have multiple options to choose from.

Dear Three Bears,

I do apologize for breaking into your home and leaving it a mess. *However*, I was lost in a scary forest and your cottage did look inviting. *In addition*, I was feeling hungry so you can't blame me for trying the porridge. I was famished! *Moreover*, I was feeling tired. I could barely keep my eyes open. *Therefore*, I did try all the beds to see which would be the most comfortable. Now, I have to say it was rather rude of you to wake me up. Though I could see you weren't happy. *Consequently* I decided to run as fast as I could. Perhaps I should have acted differently. *Nevertheless*, I should have said good day and thank you. But really, you gave me such a horrid fright that my golden locks almost turned white. How frightful! I certainly won't be coming back anytime soon!

Yours truly, Goldilocks

Note for student: Conjunctive adverbs (also known as linking adverbs) are used to link ideas, and help to show a progression of thought.

Correlative Conjunctions

A **correlative conjunction** appears in a pair. The two conjunctions support each other in a sentence.

Neither Callum **nor** Anya were able to attend the party.
You can choose **either** a hamburger **or** a hot dog.

Choose a pair of correlative conjunctions to complete these sentences. There may be more than one choice that will fit.

> either/or   neither/nor   both/and
> whether/or   not/but   not only/but also

1. I can't decide ...whether... to join the swimming team ...or... the tennis club.
2. Tomorrow, we are ...not only... going to the water park ...but also... the shopping mall.
3. Isabella can speak ...both... English ...and... Italian.
4. ...not only... was there a discount ...but also... a free gift.
5. ...neither... the twins ...nor... their friend shared the secret.
6. The detective was not sure ...either... the suspect was telling the truth ...or... lying.
7. Zara will start writing her report ...not... today ...but... tomorrow.
8. ...neither... Tommy ...nor... Jackson were chosen for the baseball team.

Note for student: Correlative conjunctions work in pairs and are helpful in connecting words and phrases within a sentence.

Commas in Lists and Clauses

You can use a **comma** to separate items in a list, or to separate clauses and ideas within a sentence. Commas, used in the correct way, make the meaning of the sentence clearer to the reader.

> Inside the treasure chest was a bag of coins, a magical potion, and a tattered map.

Commas can also separate two adjectives if you can put the word 'and' between them.

> The dragon was a large and ferocious beast.   The dragon was a large, ferocious beast.

You can use a comma when placing introductory information (a sub clause) before the main part of a sentence.

> While playing in the woods, Peter heard the sound of snapping twigs.

In a sentence, you can use commas around extra information (a sub clause) between the subject and verb.

> The brave knights, who were mounted on horses, were ready for battle.

Commas are also added before **and**, **but**, **so**, **yet**, **or**.

Correct this text by adding in the missing commas.

Troll Pest Control 101

Trolls may be intimidating, ugly, and foul-smelling adversaries, but do not despair. Follow this handy guide to help rid yourself of these troublesome, mischievous pests. You will need: a large lump of meat, some air freshener, a nose plug, and a drum or other loud instrument. The bridges, where trolls like to make their dens, are found over fast-flowing rivers. Place your meat nearby. While staying hidden, make a lot of noise to draw the troll's attention. Trolls are always hungry, so they won't be able to resist a tasty treat. While the troll is enjoying its feast, sneak under the bridge to find its den. While wearing your nose plug, because a troll den is stinky, spray your air freshener. Trolls hate nice smelling things, so when your troll returns home you can be sure they won't be sticking around!

Note for student: We use commas in writing to indicate where we take a breath or pause momentarily when reading aloud.

Commas After Tag Questions

If a sentence starts with the words yes or no, we use a comma for emphasis to set off these words from the rest of the sentence.

"No, that's not the way," said Shireen.

A comma can set off a **tag question** from the rest of a sentence. When directly addressing someone by name the comma comes before the name.

"It's true, isn't it?"   "You are very brave, Sinbad."

Correct the sentences in this story excerpt by adding the missing commas and quotation marks.

After overcoming many trials, Sinbad and his crew finally spied the ruins of an ancient city looming above the treetops.

"I was right wasn't I?" grinned Sinbad. "We made it to the city."

"Yes but I don't see any gold," said Shireen. "You promised my father riches beyond his wildest dreams."

"You must have faith Shireen," laughed Sinbad. "Have I ever let you down?"

Shireen put a finger to her chin thoughtfully. "Yes that time when I got captured by giants. Don't you remember Sinbad?"

"That's true I agree," he shrugged. "However I did come to your rescue."

"No actually I freed myself. And the time when I was stuck in that swamp."

"You have a good memory Shireen," smirked Sinbad. "This time will be different."

Shireen rolled her eyes. "Let's see Sinbad. Lead the way."

Note for student: Practice adding commas and quotation marks to dialogue by continuing the story on a separate piece of paper.

Fragments and Run-On Sentences

Each complete sentence contains a **subject** and a **predicate**.

Subject → who or what the sentence is about

Predicate → a statement about the subject

Subject → The boat | sailed across the lake. ← Predicate

If a sentence is missing a subject or a predicate then it is called a **fragment** because it is incomplete. The sentence below is missing a subject. Once we add a subject it becomes a complete sentence.

Reached the top of the hill. ← Fragment

The hikers | reached the top of the hill.

Write a complete sentence for each of the fragments below by adding a subject or a predicate.

1. The pilot of the supersonic jet…
   screamed as the plane went down into the ocean.

2. The pirate with the scowl on his face…
   stomped back up to his boat after finding no gold.

3. Cinderella…
   danced and daced with the prince untill her slippers shatered.

4. …won the Champions League.
   Messi at Real ... so that means he

5. The cruise ship…
   hit a iceberg and slowly sank down, down, down.

Note for student: Sentences should express a complete thought and contain at least one subject and one predicate. The subject refers to "who" or "what." The predicate states the action.

A **run-on** is a sentence where two or more sentences are connected without proper punctuation or a conjunction (such as: **and**, **but**, **so**, **if**, **or**, **because**, **yet**).

> Anya wants to be a vet she loves animals.

We can correct this sentence in different ways:

> Anya wants to be a vet. She loves animals. ← add punctuation

> Anya wants to be a vet **because** she loves animals. ← add a conjunction

Decide if each of these sentences contains a fragment or a run-on. Then correct the sentences by adding a subject, a predicate, or a conjunction. The first one is done for you.

1. The sun was shining we went for a walk.   fragment ○   run-on ✗
The sun was shining so we went for a walk.

2. I play the piano my brother plays the guitar.   fragment ○   run-on
I play the piano, but my brother plays the guitar

3. The car keys.   fragment   run-on ○
The car keys for a MG B were left on the sidwalk

4. The bag was heavy I packed too much.   fragment ○   run-on
The bag was heavy because I packed to much

5. The cat was frightened. Heard a loud bang.   fragment   run-on ○
The cat was frightened because she heard a loud bang

13

Connotative Language

Words can share the same meaning, but have a different feeling or intent. Depending on our choice, this can give our sentence a positive or negative connotation.

Positive connotation
Zara was **frugal** with her money.   He made a **daring** choice.

Negative connotation
Zara was **stingy** with her money.   He made a **reckless** choice.

Circle the words in the following list that imply a positive connotation. Underline the words that imply a negative connotation.

scrawny	remarkable	smirk	lazy	confused
generous	dedicated	argument	smug	cheap
creative	impulsive	stressed	demanded	stench

Read the following sentences. Replace the highlighted word with a word from the above list to give each sentence a negative connotation.

1. My friend listened to my story then gave a **smile** (…………………).

2. There was a big **debate** (…………………) about who should do the washing up.

3. Kelly **asked** (…………………) that everyone be quiet.

4. The ending of the film has left me **puzzled** (…………………).

5. Harry was **confident** (…………………) because he knew the answer.

6. The candles gave off a strong **fragrance** (…………………).

7. Mary is very **relaxed** (…………………) when it comes to tidying up.

8. The **slender** (…………………) black cat crept along the wall.

Note for student: Reread the sentences and consider how the author's feeling and intent has changed by using a different word with a similar meaning.

Formal and Informal Language

We often change the way we write or speak depending on who our audience is, and the type of information we want to communicate.

Informal language is used when speaking or writing to people we are close to or familiar with, such as friends and family. Written examples might include journals, text messages, emails, and social media posts.

Formal language is used when speaking or writing to someone we don't know, or someone we want to impress or show respect to. Written examples might include essays, reports, instructions, or important letters.

Check ✔ the box to show whether the following sentences are formal or informal.

1. For safety reasons, please refrain from running in the school corridors. ⬡ Formal ⬡ Informal
2. While the chocolate is melting, combine the caramel with the sea salt in a separate bowl. ⬡ Formal ⬡ Informal
3. I can't believe you can lift that! You've got way too much stuff in your suitcase. ⬡ Formal ⬡ Informal
4. Hey, everyone, please check out my latest video. I share heaps of tips on how to save money! ⬡ Formal ⬡ Informal
5. I am writing to inform you about the recent incident concerning the stolen purse. ⬡ Formal ⬡ Informal

Tom has drafted the following article for his school magazine. Help him to improve his informal sentences by using formal language.

So last Friday (March 20) was really cool cos sixth grade got to do "The Book Run" to get cash to pay for the new school library. Kids ran 4 laps of the school fields. It rained and it was super muddy but sixth grade stuck with it and everyone finished. The sixth grade is awesome!

....

....

....

Note for student: Formal language avoids slang terms, abbreviated words, contractions (e.g. don't/shouldn't), and figures of speech.

Treasure Island

Read the following excerpt from *Treasure Island* by Robert Louis Stevenson.

Chapter 1: The Old Sea-Dog at the "Admiral Benbow"

Squire Trelawney, Dr. Livesey, and the rest of these gentlemen having asked me to write down the whole particulars about Treasure Island, from the beginning to the end, keeping nothing back but the bearings of the island, and that only because there is still treasure not yet lifted, I take up my pen in the year of grace 17—, and go back to the time when my father kept the Admiral Benbow Inn and the brown old seaman with the sabre cut first took up his lodging under our roof.

I remember him as if it were yesterday, as he came plodding to the inn door, his sea-chest following behind him in a hand-barrow—a tall, strong, heavy, nut-brown man, his tarry pigtail falling over the shoulder of his soiled blue coat, his hands ragged and scarred, with black, broken nails, and the sabre cut across one cheek, a dirty, livid white. I remember him looking round the cove and whistling to himself as he did so, and then breaking out in that old sea-song that he sang so often afterwards:

*"Fifteen men on the dead man's chest—
Yo-ho-ho, and a bottle of rum!"*

in the high, old tottering voice that seemed to have been tuned and broken at the capstan bars. Then he rapped on the door with a bit of stick like a handspike that he carried, and when my father appeared, called roughly for a glass of rum. This, when it was brought to him, he drank slowly, like a connoisseur, lingering on the taste and still looking about him at the cliffs and up at our signboard.

Note for student: *Treasure Island* is the story of a twelve-year-old boy, Jim Hawkins, who discovers a map that leads to pirate treasure. The book was first published in 1883.

"This is a handy cove," says he at length; "and a pleasant sittyated grog-shop. Much company, mate?"

My father told him no, very little company, the more was the pity.

"Well, then," said he, "this is the berth for me. Here you, matey," he cried to the man who trundled the barrow; "bring up alongside and help up my chest. I'll stay here a bit," he continued. "I'm a plain man; rum and bacon and eggs is what I want, and that head up there for to watch ships off. What you mought call me? You mought call me captain. Oh, I see what you're at—there"; and he threw down three or four gold pieces on the threshold. "You can tell me when I've worked through that," says he, looking as fierce as a commander.

And indeed bad as his clothes were and coarsely as he spoke, he had none of the appearance of a man who sailed before the mast, but seemed like a mate or skipper accustomed to be obeyed or to strike. The man who came with the barrow told us the mail had set him down the morning before at the Royal George, that he had inquired what inns there were along the coast, and hearing ours well spoken of, I suppose, and described as lonely, had chosen it from the others for his place of residence. And that was all we could learn of our guest.

Responding to Treasure Island

Read the excerpt on the previous pages before answering the questions.

1. Who is narrating the story? Check ✔ your answer.

   ☐ Dr. Livesey   ☐ The innkeeper's son   ☐ The Captain   ☐ Squire Trelawney

   What evidence in the text supports your answer?

   ....

   ....

   Treasure Island is written in the first person: the events are recounted through the eyes of one of the characters. Note the use of the pronouns I, my, we, and our in the text.

2. Refer to the title of the chapter excerpt on page 60. Who is the "Old Sea-Dog?"

   ....

3. Match these words from the text with their meanings. Locate the words in the text and look for context clues to help you.

Word	
berth	......6......
connoisseur	....
grog-shop	....
more was the pity	....
mought	....
sittyated	....
skipper	....
threshold	....

   Meanings
   1. (n.) an inn
   2. (adv.) unfortunately
   3. (v.) situated
   4. (n.) the bottom of a doorway
   5. (n.) captain of a ship or boat
   6. (n.) a sleeping place
   7. (v.) might
   8. (n.) an expert in taste

Note for student: Look for clues in the text to help you figure out the meaning of unfamiliar words.

4. How does the author describe the scar on the Captain's face? Quote directly from the text.

   ....

5. Replace the bold words in these sentences with synonyms:

   When referring to the Captain: "… seemed like a mate or skipper **accustomed to** be obeyed."

   "accustomed to" could be replaced with ....

   "…these gentlemen having asked me to write down the **whole particulars** about Treasure Island, from the beginning to the end…"

   "whole particulars" could be replaced with ....

   "…he cried to the man who **trundled** the barrow…"

   "trundled" could be replaced with ....

6. What can we infer from the text about the character who calls himself the "Captain?" Look for evidence in the text to support the following viewpoints.

   He is in hiding and doesn't want to be found.

   ....

   ....

   He is looking for someone.

   ....

   ....

Raven Steals the Light

A Native American Myth

At the very beginning of time, the world was in darkness. There was no sun, nor moon, nor stars. The land was a barren, gray wilderness, devoid of color and life. Raven was the first animal, alone in this dark world. He was frustrated that even his bright eyes could not pierce the gloom. He would often find himself flying into trees and rocks, his black coat dishevelled by all his bumps and scrapes.

Near the mountains, there lived an old and miserly man known as Sky Father who had a daughter. Each day she would weep, for she was very sad. She wanted a husband to marry, but with no light in the world, she could not find him.

Raven heard her weeping and was drawn to the wood cabin where Sky Father lived. He had sharp hearing, which made up for his poor sight. When the daughter left the cabin to go and collect water from the nearby stream, he heard Sky Father muttering to himself.

"All the light in the world is mine," he sniggered. "All locked away in this little box, which I will hide inside another box, inside another box, inside another box. No one will ever find it. As long as there is darkness, my daughter will never leave me."

Raven started to hatch a plan to trick Sky Father and steal the light.

He flew down to where the chuckling river wound through the valley. The daughter was dipping her bucket in the water. Raven quickly transformed himself into a hemlock needle and dropped into the water. He was scooped up into the daughter's bucket. When she took a sip of the refreshing mountain water, she unknowingly swallowed the hemlock needle. It slid into her belly where it started to grow, transforming itself into an unborn baby.

Forty weeks later, the daughter gave birth to a baby boy. He was a very strange-looking baby. Although the world was in darkness, she could see his shining eyes and feel the feathers on his skin. This was a raven baby. He would bawl and wail, always demanding attention. Then as a child, when he could speak in the soft sing-song tones of Raven, he begged Sky Father for a toy to play with.

Note for student: Raven appears in many of the creation stories of the indigenous people of the Pacific Northwest. He is a trickster character whose actions change the world.

"I have no toys for you," grumbled Sky Father.

The raven child was persistent, begging and whining until Sky Father finally gave in.

"Okay. Take this box to play with," he grunted, handing over the box.

Raven Child opened the box, and the next box, and the next—until he had the little box in his hands. Before Sky Father could stop him, Raven Child threw open the little box, revealing a bright orb of dazzling brilliance. With a loud cawing, the child transformed back into Raven and snatched up the orb in his claws. He immediately took to flight, wings beating fast.

Sky Father fell into a furious rage. He turned himself into a giant eagle and chased Raven. "Give me back the light!" he screeched.

Raven was not the fastest of fliers and the heavy orb was weighing him down. He broke off some of the light, scattering it across the heavens. The first stars twinkled into existence. But he was still too slow. He broke off another piece, creating the pale moon. By the light of its soft radiance, Raven could finally see the horizon. He flew as fast as he could, but the eagle was still faster. Weak and tired, Raven grudgingly let go of his treasure. It fell into the ocean, then began to rise again as a dazzling sun—bringing light to all the world.

Sky Father angrily returned to his cabin to find his daughter had gone. By the light of the sun, she had finally found her husband. Together, they had many happy children who would become the first tribe on earth.

Responding to Raven Steals the Light

Read the myth of *Raven Steals the Light* on the previous pages before answering the questions below.

1. What is Sky Father hiding inside the little box?
   ....

2. How do we know that Sky Father's daughter is unhappy?
   ....

3. What is Raven's plan to trick Sky Father?
   ....
   ....

4. Do you think Raven was right to steal something that did not belong to him? Explain your answer.
   ....
   ....

5. Do you think the narrator is sympathetic to Raven or Sky Father? Use evidence from the text to support your opinion.
   ....
   ....
   ....

Note for student: This activity encourages you to explore a narrator's or speaker's point of view, and reflect on how this can influence the way events are described in a story.

Read this alternative opening to the story, told from the point of view of Sky Father.

> Since the loss of my dear wife, I only have my daughter for company. I know she is lonely and I fear she may leave me to find a husband. She is all I have left. If she leaves me then I will be alone in the world. That is my biggest fear. So, I have taken all the light and I am keeping it safe inside a little box. It's only fair that I look after it, as I created it in the first place. No one else deserves to have it.

6. What new information does this paragraph tell us about Sky Father?

   ....
   ....
   ....

7. Write a paragraph of your own to describe the moment when Raven steals the light, told from the point of view of Sky Father.

   ....
   ....
   ....
   ....
   ....
   ....
   ....

Remarkable Eyes

 **Compare and Contrast**

Read about the incredible ways in which some animals are able to view the world.

Eagle Eyes
The bald eagle has the best vision of all in the animal kingdom. Its eyes are the same size as a human eyeball and weigh more than its brain. They are fixed in their sockets, unlike human eyeballs which can move, so the eagle must turn its head to survey its surroundings. Compared to humans, the eagle has a larger range of vision, with two focal points (unlike a human's singular **focal point**) that allow it to see straight ahead and to the side at the same time. The eagle also has incredible depth of vision, and can focus on details at a great distance. A bald eagle can see a rabbit from over 3 miles away!
Amazing fact! Eagles have a third eyelid. This thin **membrane** sweeps across the eye from side to side, similar to a windshield wiper, and helps keep the eye moist and clean.

Glossary
focal point: what the eye is able to concentrate on
membrane: a thin layer or covering

human (180 degrees)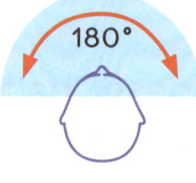

bald eagle (340 degrees)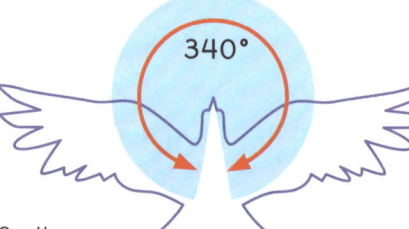

dragonfly (360 degrees)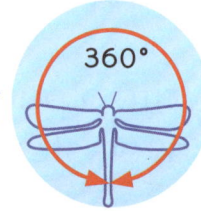

Airborne Hunters
Dragonflies have the largest compound eyes of all insects. Compound eyes are made up of thousands of tiny lenses. Each lens captures a separate image, which is sent to the insect's brain where it puts them all together to create one big picture. The dragonfly's eyes cover most of its head and provide a stunning 360-degree angle of its surroundings—but, unlike the bald eagle, it is nearsighted and cannot see at a great distance. Because its eyes are fixed in place, a dragonfly must turn its head if it wants to change its angle of vision. Most of its prey are smaller flying insects, so dragonfly eyes see faster than other eyes and are able to track fast-moving prey with ease.
Amazing fact! Both the dragonfly and the bald eagle can see more colors than a human, including ultraviolet light.

Note for student: This activity encourages you to look for similarities and differences between different subjects.

Eyes on the Move

The chameleon has a very unique pair of eyes. Each eye can move independently of the other, which means the chameleon can look in different directions at once! This allows it to search out prey quickly and easily. When it spots a tasty meal, both eyes point forward focusing on their target so that the chameleon can judge distance better and catch its prey on the end of its long sticky tongue!

Amazing Fact!

Chameleons have a single cone-shaped eyelid which covers the entire eyeball, leaving only a tiny slit for the pupil to see out of. However, like the bald eagle, the chameleon has a special membrane that sweeps across the eye to keep it clean and moist.

Predator or Prey?

A predator is an animal that hunts and eats other animals for food. Prey is the term used to describe an animal that is hunted. The position of an animal's eyes can help us to judge whether it is a predator or prey.

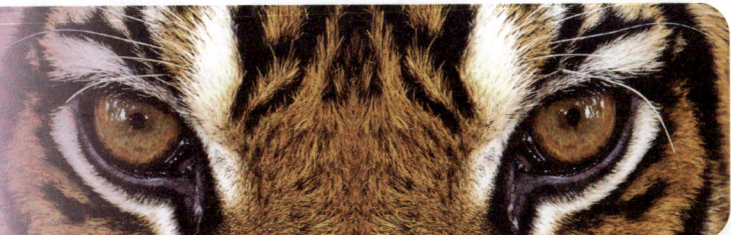

Predators have forward-facing eyes, which allow them to see and judge distances more easily, so they can track and chase their prey.

Prey animals have eyes positioned at the side of their heads, providing them with a wider panoramic view of their surroundings. This can alert them to dangers such as incoming predators.

Remember:
Eyes at the front, likes to hunt.
Eyes at the side, likes to hide.

Comparing Information

Compare and Contrast

When we are asked to compare and contrast two subjects, we are looking for their similarities and differences. By reading the nonfiction text on the previous pages, we can identify facts and record these in a Venn diagram.

How are a bald eagle's eyes similar to and/or different from a human's eyes?

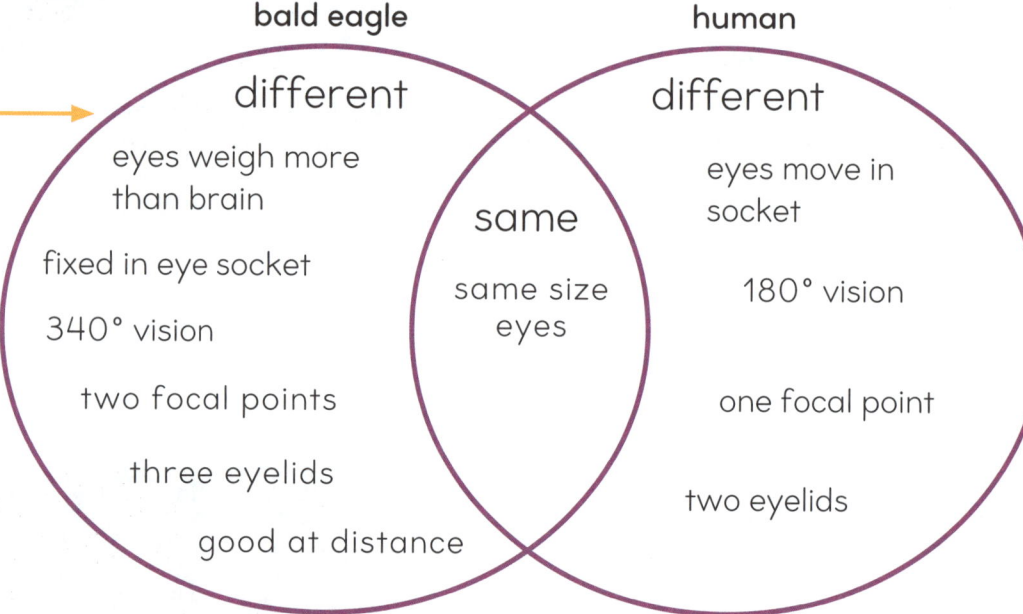

bald eagle — different
- eyes weigh more than brain
- fixed in eye socket
- 340° vision
- two focal points
- three eyelids
- good at distance

same
- same size eyes

human — different
- eyes move in socket
- 180° vision
- one focal point
- two eyelids

How are a bald eagle's eyes similar to and/or different from a dragonfly's eyes?

Use the facts from the nonfiction text to help you complete this Venn diagram.

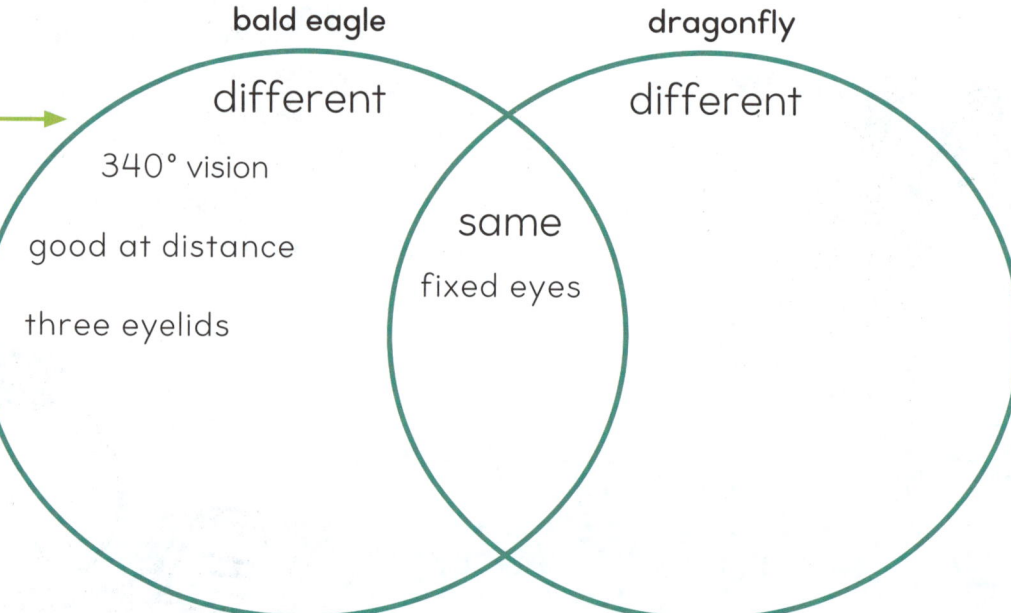

bald eagle — different
- 340° vision
- good at distance
- three eyelids

same
- fixed eyes

dragonfly — different

Note for student: A graphic organizer, such as a Venn diagram, can help you to organize your notes and visualize information.

Use the nonfiction text on the previous pages to help you complete the following statements.

1. Both the .... and the ....
have a special membrane that helps to keep their eyes clean and moist.

2. Unlike the bald eagle and the ...., the eyes of the
.... can move in their sockets and look in different directions.

3. Humans have a single .... whereas a bald eagle has two.

4. In contrast to the eyes of the bald eagle, those of the ....
cannot see great distances.

Label these animal images as predator or prey based on what you have learned from the text.

lion

zebra

jack rabbit

....

deer

coyote

red fox

....

27

Louis Braille Biography

Read the biography of Louis Braille then answer the questions.

Louis Braille was born in Coupvray near Paris in 1809. His father owned a harness shop making leather harnesses for horses. At the age of three, Louis was playing with the tools in his father's workshop when he accidentally scratched his eye. Despite treatment, the eye became infected and that infection gradually spread to the other eye. By the age of five, Louis was blind in both eyes.

Louis's parents were very supportive and encouraged him to attend school. Louis was a bright student and by the age of ten he was offered a place at the Royal Institute for Blind Youth in Paris where he could learn many subjects, such as history, geography, grammar, and math.

The Royal Institute was founded by Valentin Haüy, who had invented his own method of making books for the blind. This method involved stamping large letter plates into soft, damp paper to leave a raised impression. Because the letters were big, a sentence could take up a whole page—this would mean that the books would be very large and heavy. Also, the letters were so big that it could take a long time to feel them and put the words together.

Louis was frustrated because he wanted to read as quickly as sighted people. He learned of a system invented by Charles Barbier, a captain in the French army. Barbier created a way for soldiers to send messages to each other at night without needing light or having to talk. His system used a heavy tool to punch dots into paper. These represented letters and sounds, which could be put together to make words. It was complicated to learn and difficult to use.

Louis worked hard to improve Barbier's system and eventually devised his own version. Students at the institute tried out the new "Braille" system and they immediately found it easier to learn and quicker to read. They could even take notes in class!

Louis eventually became a full-time teacher at the institute and spent a lot of time copying books into his special code. Sadly, his health began to deteriorate and in 1835 he was diagnosed with tuberculosis, a disease of the lungs. He died in January 1852.

Two years later Braille became the standard reading method for the blind in France, and in 1878 the World Congress for the Blind voted to make Braille the reading system for all blind people around the world.

Note for student: This activity requires the study of different sources of information (biography, illustration, and timeline) in order to develop an understanding of the topic.

| 1809 Louis Braille is born in France. | 1814 Louis is blind in both eyes. | 1822 Louis discovers the Barbier system. | 1824 Louis reveals his new system. | 1829 Louis publishes his first book. | 1852 Louis dies at 43. |

Louis improved the Barbier system by reducing the number of dots. His version also included all of the letters of the alphabet, as well as numbers and punctuation marks.

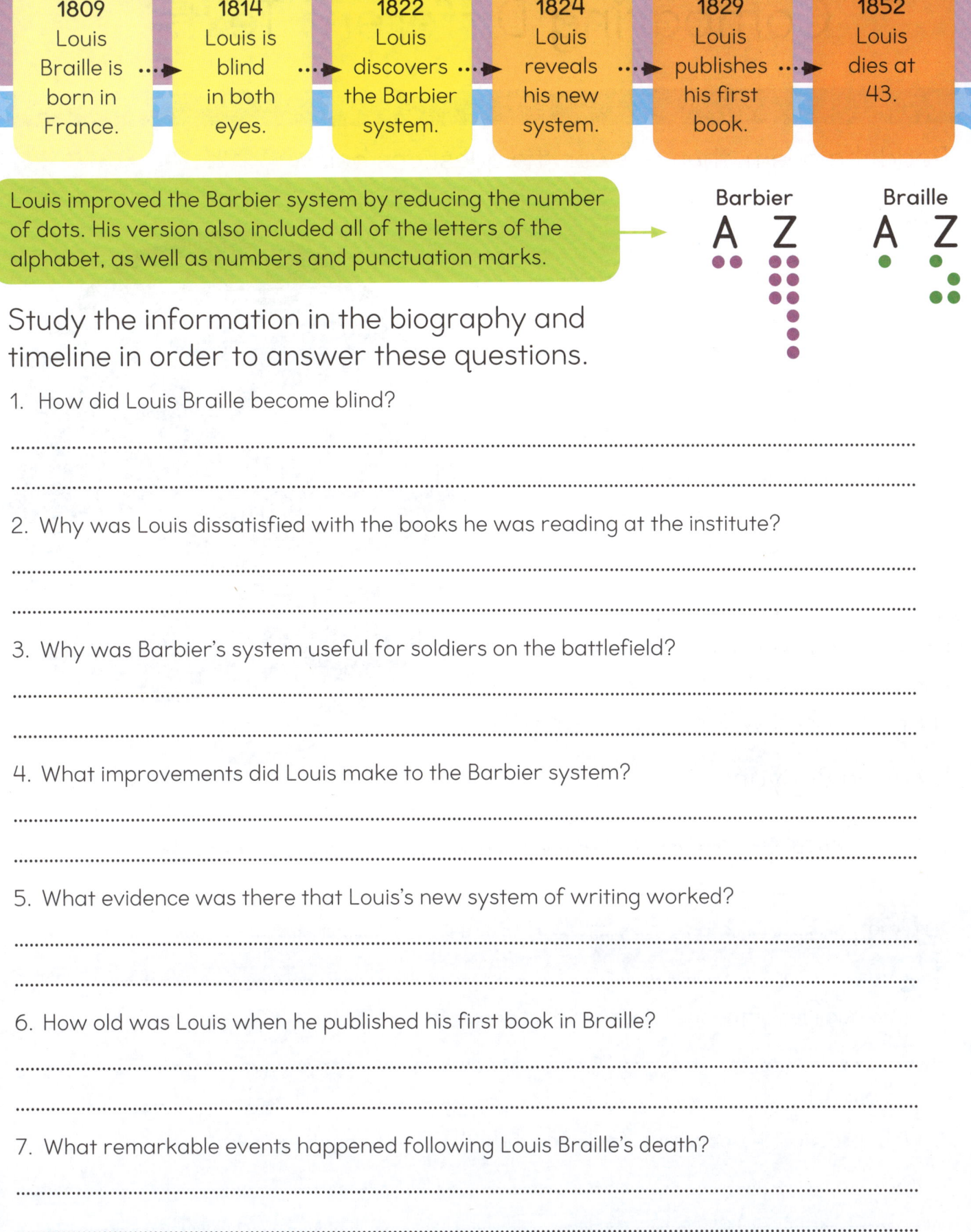

Study the information in the biography and timeline in order to answer these questions.

1. How did Louis Braille become blind?

....

....

2. Why was Louis dissatisfied with the books he was reading at the institute?

....

....

3. Why was Barbier's system useful for soldiers on the battlefield?

....

....

4. What improvements did Louis make to the Barbier system?

....

....

5. What evidence was there that Louis's new system of writing worked?

....

....

6. How old was Louis when he published his first book in Braille?

....

....

7. What remarkable events happened following Louis Braille's death?

....

....

Comparing Different Texts

Read the poem, then answer the questions below.

Upon A Snail

She goes but softly, but she goeth sure,
She stumbles not, as stronger creatures do;
Her journey's shorter, so she may endure
Better than they which do much further go.

She makes no noise, but stilly seizeth on
The flower or herb appointed for her food;
The which she quietly doth feed upon,
While others range and glare, but find no good.

And though she doth but very softly go,
However slow her pace be, yet 'tis sure;
And certainly they that do travel so,
The prize which they do aim at, they procure.

By John Bunyan

1. Write a definition for each of the highlighted words, using context clues to help you.

   seizeth ....
   range ....
   procure ....

2. What qualities of the snail does the poet admire?
   ....
   ....

3. What practical lesson about life do you think the poet is teaching us?
   ....
   ....

Note for student: Remember to make specific reference to the texts when supporting your responses. Use extra paper if needed to extend your answers.

Read the story excerpt then answer the questions below.

The animals scrambled ashore, the remains of their boat now ruined amongst the rocks. Captain Hare was naturally furious at this turn of events, his ears twitching frantically. "That's the last time we put Mole on lookout!" he snapped.

"I told you I had terrible sight…" whimpered Mole, but Hare wasn't listening.

"The storm is coming and we're shipwrecked!" he cried, hopping around madly. "It's all a hopeless mess!" He continued in this way for some time, his words only serving to sow further panic amongst the animals.

"We should make a den!" cried Mouse.

"No, repair the ship!" clucked Hen.

"Find food!" sniffled Hedgehog.

Every animal had their own hasty plan, but no one seemed to be achieving much, except getting in each other's way.

And no one had paid any attention to Snail—her quiet, calm voice having gone unheard. With a shrug of her tiny shell, she slowly slid herself onto a nearby rock and started to patiently act out her own plan.

An hour passed and dark clouds were tumbling overhead. The animals were hopelessly exhausted after their failed efforts and too tired to even moan about their predicament.

But Snail had stuck to her plan. When the moon appeared briefly between the clouds, full and bright, its light shone on the glittering slime trail that Snail had made—spelling out the word 'Help!' And it was this that caught the attention of the passing Blue Jay who swooped down to offer her aid.

1. How does Snail's approach differ from that of the other animals?
....
....

2. Do you think the poet of "Upon A Snail" and the writer of this story share similar viewpoints? Give evidence using examples from both texts.
....
....
....

Jabberwocky

When you read the poem "Jabberwocky" you will see that many words are nonsense words. Try to figure out their meaning by using context clues and/or by looking for "portmanteau" words.

Portmanteau words are made up from the parts of other words. "Slithy" is a combination of lithe and slimy. Portmanteau is French for a large travel bag!

Some words in the poem are real words you might be unfamiliar with. Write a definition for these highlighted words then check your answers using a dictionary.

gyre ....
....

shun ....
....

foe ....
....

burbled ....
....

galumphing ....
....

chortled ....
....

'Twas brillig, and the slithy toves
Did gyre and gimble in the wabe;
All mimsy were the borogoves,
And the mome raths outgrabe.

"Beware the Jabberwock, my son!
The jaws that bite, the claws that catch!
Beware the Jubjub bird, and shun
The frumious Bandersnatch!"

He took his vorpal sword in hand:
Long time the manxome foe he sought
So rested he by the Tumtum tree,
And stood awhile in thought.

And as in uffish thought he stood,
The Jabberwock, with eyes of flame,
Came whiffling through the tulgey wood,
And burbled as it came!

One, two! One, two! And through and through
The vorpal blade went snicker-snack!
He left it dead, and with its head
He went galumphing back.

"And hast thou slain the Jabberwock?
Come to my arms, my beamish boy!
O frabjous day! Callooh! Callay!"
He chortled in his joy.

'Twas brillig, and the slithy toves
Did gyre and gimble in the wabe;
All mimsy were the borogoves,
And the mome raths outgrabe.

By Lewis Carroll

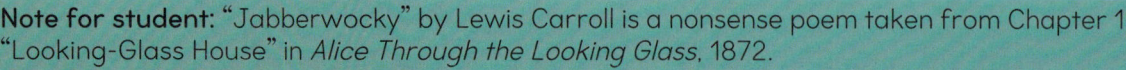
Note for student: "Jabberwocky" by Lewis Carroll is a nonsense poem taken from Chapter 1: "Looking-Glass House" in *Alice Through the Looking Glass*, 1872.

1. What do the words "slithy toves did gyre" suggest to you about the setting for the poem? Think about what things whirl or gyrate in the natural world. State evidence from the text to support your answer.

....

....

2. In stanza 2, the Bandersnatch is described as frumious. This portmanteau word is created from the parts of two other words:

   fuming **+** furious **=** frumious   to mean **angry**

   Create your own portmanteau words to match these definitions.

   .... **+** .... **=** ....   to mean **hungry**
   .... **+** .... **=** ....   to mean **gigantic**
   .... **+** .... **=** ....   to mean **terrifying**

3. What might the boy be thinking in stanza 3, as he rests by the Tumtum tree?

....

....

4. In stanza 4, replace the nonsense words with real words:

uffish thought ....   came whiffling ....

tulgey wood ....

5. Summarize what happens in stanzas 5 and 6.

....

....

....

6. What do you think "O frabjous day! Collooh! Callay!" means?

....

....

33

Making a Claim

Read the following argument then answer the questions.

Everyone Needs Exercise!

I've noticed that some children my age have a negative view of exercise. If they don't like sports, then they think exercise is not for them. However, I think regular exercise is really important. Not only is it great for the mind and body, but it can be fun, too!

First of all, it is crucial to know that exercise is good for all parts of our body. We all know that exercise gets the heart pumping and the lungs working harder. This is great for our physical health because studies show that regular exercise can reduce the risk of many serious illnesses, such as diabetes and heart disease. However, did you know that exercise also improves the brain? In a study done at the University of British Columbia, researchers found that exercise helps boost the brain area responsible for memory and learning. That means exercise can even help you with your school work!

In addition, exercise can give a real sense of accomplishment. I started out by setting myself realistic goals—such as learning a new dance routine—and when I achieved these I felt proud of myself. This was really good for my self-esteem because it taught me not to be afraid of new things. Learning this has helped me in other areas of my life too, such as moving to a different state. I was nervous but I tried hard to settle in and make new friends, and now I am loving my new school.

Some children think that exercise is boring, but in my opinion this doesn't have to be the case. Choose an activity that interests you. It could be learning to mountain bike, trying out indoor rock climbing, or even teaching yourself to hula-hoop! I have always loved dancing so I started classes and I have learned lots of new styles, such as jazz and hip hop.

In conclusion, there are lots of benefits to doing exercise and I'd encourage everyone to consider what they could do to introduce exercise into their lives. You might even have some fun along the way!

Jayden, age 11

Note for student: A claim is an author's position or viewpoint on a topic. Evidence is the information, such as facts, anecdotes, quotes or data, that help to support the claim.

1. What is the author's main claim (point of view) in the article?
   ....
   ....

2. What is the author's reason for writing this article?
   ....
   ....

3. What evidence does the author provide to support each of these reasons:

Exercise is good for physical health.	....
Exercise improves brain health.	....
Exercise improves self-esteem.	....

4. What counter argument does the author raise in this article and how do they answer it?
   ....
   ....

5. Do you agree or disagree with the author's point of view? Explain your answer.
   ....
   ....
   ....

Writing

Student Notes

The activities in this section will help you learn how to:

- Develop and practice your writing skills.
- Write your own poems and improve your own imaginative stories.
- Produce clear and coherent writing to convey ideas and information, and to support an argument.

You may choose to work on the activities independently, or you may want help from a parent or other adult at the start of an activity.

Contents

Writing Paragraphs	38
Transitions Within Paragraphs	39
Titles, Subheadings, Captions, and Labels	40
Supporting Details	41
Planning a History Report	42
Writing a History Report	44
Planning an Argument	46
Writing an Argument	48
Writing Poetry	50
Similes and Metaphors	51
Personification	52
Poem Structure	54
Story Structure	56
Who Tells the Story	58
Story Plot	59
Writing a Scene	60
Answers	124

Writing Paragraphs

When writing an instructional text, we group sentences that share a common idea into paragraphs. There are three parts to a paragraph.

The topic sentence introduces what the paragraph will be about.

The supporting details provide examples that support the main idea of the paragraph.

The concluding sentence restates or summarizes the main idea of the paragraph.

Space technology can do some amazing things! For example, did you know there is a flying telescope orbiting the Earth, which can see some of the most distant objects in the universe? Not only that, there is also a manned space station in orbit where scientists can conduct experiments in zero gravity. This amazing technology helps us every day to learn more about outer space.

Reorder and rewrite these jumbled sentences to make a complete paragraph.

- It is surrounded by rings of rock and ice.
- Saturn is known as the ringed planet.
- The rings make Saturn a fascinating planet.
- They can be seen from Earth with a telescope.

Topic sentence:

....

Supporting detail one:

....

Supporting detail two:

....

Concluding sentence:

....

Note for student: This activity provides practice in structuring a paragraph for an informational text, with a main idea supported by facts and details.

Transitions Within Paragraphs

Transitions are words or phrases that connect ideas. They help writing to flow from one sentence to another. Here are some examples of common transitions.

To show time or sequence:
First   Finally   Previously
Then   Meanwhile   After
Next   Later   Eventually

To add information or examples:
For example   Furthermore   As well
Such as   Additionally   In fact
For instance   Also   Like

To conclude:
In conclusion   In closing
Therefore   Obviously
Thus   In summary

To compare or contrast:
By comparison   Similarly   Also
On the other hand   Compared to   Although
In the same way   In contrast to   However

Underline the transitions in the paragraph below.

When it's too dark to see, we simply flick a switch. However, the invention of the light bulb took many years to perfect. First, English scientist Humphrey Davy invented the arc lamp. Although the invention worked, it was far too large and dangerous to be used in the home. Therefore, inventors had to come up with a better idea. Finally, around 1850, two scientists, Thomas Edison and Joseph Swan, simultaneously developed a safe working light bulb. Initially, they argued over who had invented it first, but eventually they settled their differences and worked together. Thus, they were able to refine their designs and bring light to the world!

Note for student: Transitions connect ideas within and between paragraphs to help writing flow. Without them, writing sounds like a list instead of related ideas.

Titles, Subheadings, Captions, and Labels

Informational text uses titles and subheadings to group sentences together in the correct order. Illustrations or diagrams, with captions and labels, are used to help comprehension. Complete this history report by writing an appropriate title and subheadings.

Title: ....
A nighttime encounter with a stray cat gave one inventor a brilliant idea—to develop a device that would make our roads safer for drivers.

Subheading: ....
One dark, foggy night in 1933, English inventor Percy Shaw was driving home. The road was steep and winding and Shaw couldn't see very well. He nearly drove off the road and over a cliff. He was saved because he saw two small lights by the roadside. They were the eyes of a stray cat reflected in his car headlights. Those lights saved his life by helping him to stay away from the road's edge. This gave Shaw a brilliant idea.

Subheading: ....
Shaw decided to make a reflector that would mark the sides of the road at night. The reflector had glass balls, similar to a cat's eyes. When light shone into the glass balls, the reflective backing would bounce the light back. Shaw patented his invention in 1934 to protect his idea and stop others from copying it.

Subheading: ....
In 1937, the British government ran a competition to find the best road reflector. Shaw's invention won and soon his factory was manufacturing "cat's eyes" for roads all across Britain. They were so successful at reducing accidents that many roads around the world have their own set of cat's eyes today. This simple invention may have saved thousands of lives!

Write a caption for the diagram below.

....

A cat's shining eyes are caused by a silvery layer of cells behind the retina. These cells are called the tapetum lucidum (Latin for "bright tapestry"). These act like a mirror, bouncing light back against the retina to give cats better night vision.

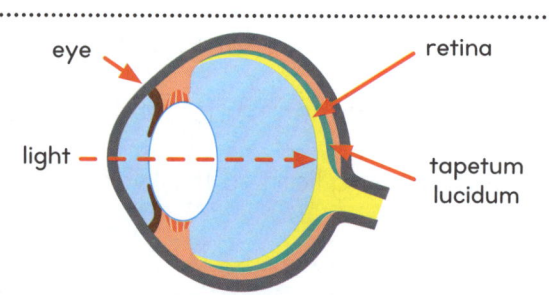

Note for student: Information and ideas can be structured using headings, subheadings, paragraphs, illustrations, and diagrams.

Supporting Details

In informational texts, supporting details help explain or support the main idea. These details can be provided using quotations, facts, and definitions related to the topic. Read the history report on the opposite page, then answer the following questions.

What is the main idea of the text? Check ✔ your answer.

A ☐ Driving at night can be dangerous.

B ☐ Cat's eyes are an amazing invention that led to safer roads.

C ☐ A cat's eyes glow in the dark.

D ☐ Brilliant ideas can make you famous.

What three details below support the main idea? Check ✔ your answer.

A ☐ "This simple invention may have saved thousands of lives!"

B ☐ "A cat's shining eyes are caused by a silvery layer of cells…"

C ☐ "…the British government ran a competition to find the best road reflector."

D ☐ "They were so successful at reducing accidents…"

E ☐ "Those lights saved his life by helping him to stay away from the road's edge."

Write a definition for each word or term.

tapetum lucidum ....

patent ....

Which of the following quotations would best support the text about cat's eyes? Check ✔ your answer.

☐ "They light the way, shining through dust and dirt and fog… showing the world's night drivers the safe way home." Alan Whicker, journalist.

☐ "It was that foggy that the headlights just make a white sheet. You can't see nothing." Percy Shaw, inventor.

Note for student: The main idea represents the central theme or purpose of the entire text. The supporting details help to explain, describe, and illustrate the main idea.

Planning a History Report

To research a topic, it is important to build your knowledge by looking at different sources. These could be books, websites, magazine or newspaper articles, videos, and so on. These sources can be listed in a bibliography so that your reader can see where you researched your facts.

When writing a bibliography, sources are listed in a particular way.

For a book:
author's last name, author's first name. *Title of book*. Publisher, date.
Jackson, Paul. *The Night Sky*. New Moon Books, 2014.

For an article:
author's last name, author's first name. "Title of article." *Name of publication*. Date.
Arain, Hanif. "Thank the Aztecs for Chocolate!" *The History Magazine*. November 16, 2021.

For a website:
author's last name, author's first name. "Title of article." Date recorded. Website URL.
Bouman, Katie. "How to Take a Picture of a Black Hole."
Filmed November 2016 at TEDxBeaconStreet, Brookline, MA. Video, 12:51.
https://www.ted.com/talks/katie_bouman_what_does_a_black_hole_look_like

Choose a history topic to research. Here are some suggestions.

The History of Chocolate   Famous Astronomers

Find three different sources that will help you research your topic. Write your sources in the bibliography below.

Bibliography

1. ....
2. ....
3. ....

Note for student: Remember to always write ideas in your own words rather than copying word-for-word from a source.

For each of your sources, note some of the facts you have learned. When taking notes, remember to write in your own words so you are not copying the author's exact words.

Source 1 ....
....
....
....
....
....

Remember to record important dates and events.

Source 2 ....
....
....
....
....
....

Choose facts that support your main idea or topic.

Source 3 ....
....
....
....
....
....

Notes are just reminders. They don't have to be perfect sentences.

Writing a History Report

When we write about history we write in chronological (time) order and include any important dates and events. We write in past tense and third person.

History of the Potato Chip

In the 1850s, the Moon Lake House in New York was a popular restaurant for the very wealthy. In 1853, one fussy diner named Cornelius Vanderbilt ordered some french fries, but when they were served, he was not happy. He sent them straight back to the kitchen, demanding that they be thinner and crispier! The chef, George Crum, made some more but they were still not thin enough. George was so annoyed with his difficult customer that he sliced a potato as thinly as he could, and overcooked the slices until brown and crispy. The customer loved them—and soon everyone wanted to try George Crum's ultrathin fries.

In 1895, William Tappendon turned his barn in Cleveland, Ohio into the world's first potato chip factory. He was so successful that many other factories started to spring up across America. Now people could buy chips in handy tins or tubs. They had become a snack that could be enjoyed on the move.

It was not until 1926 that the chip bag was invented. Factory owner Laura Scudder noticed that her chips would go stale quickly. To solve the problem, she began making bags out of wax paper, sealed with a hot iron. Today, chip bags are still made in a similar way, but use plastic instead of paper.

Up until the 1950s, potato chips came with a bag of salt to flavor them. In 1954, Joe Murphy, an Irish chip manufacturer, decided to experiment with other flavors. His company, Tayto, was the first to develop salt and vinegar, and cheese and onion flavored chips. His ideas paved the way for other companies to try out their own flavors—revolutionizing the world of the potato chip forever!

Note for student: Transitional words (such as: after, before, until, therefore, soon, etc.) are helpful in linking sentences and ideas together.

Use the information in the history report to complete this timeline. Write the facts in your own words.

1853 George Crum invented potato chips to please a customer.

1895 ....

1926 ....

1954 ....

Now write your own history report using the notes you prepared on pages 42-43.

....
....
....
....
....
....
....
....
....
....
....
....

You may want to use additional paper to complete your report and include a timeline.

Planning an Argument

You can share your viewpoint on a topic by writing an argument.

> An argument aims to win over the reader to your viewpoint. A strong argument should consist of clear reasons that state your case, and reliable evidence to support those reasons.

When we write an argument, we first decide on the claim that we want to make.

My main claim	This communicates your viewpoint plainly. Often this will form the title for your argument.

You can then organize your thoughts into the following sections:

Introduction	Grab the reader's attention with a strong statement that will introduce the topic. State your main claim (viewpoint) to prepare the reader for your argument.
Reasons	Give strong reasons as to why you have arrived at your viewpoint.
Evidence	Back up each reason with relevant and reliable evidence that supports your viewpoint. Evidence could include facts, quotes, or data.
Counter argument	Show your reader that you are aware that others will have a different viewpoint to your own.
Rebuttal	Answer the counter argument with strong evidence that supports your claim and challenges the opposing viewpoint.
Conclusion	Remind the reader of your claim and summarize your reasons. End with a strong final statement for your reader to think about.

Now plan an argument to share your own viewpoint on one of the following topics.

- e-books should replace physical books
- vending machines should ban junk food
- animals should not be kept in a zoo

Note for student: You may wish to read Making a Claim on pages 34-35, and the example viewpoint on pages 48-49, for ideas on organizing and planning your own argument.

Use the following graphic organizer to help you plan out the parts of your argument.

My main claim ....

Introduction
....
....
....

Reason
....
....
....

Evidence
....
....
....

Reason
....
....
....

Evidence
....
....
....

Counter argument
....
....
....

Rebuttal
....
....
....

Conclusion
....
....
....

Writing an Argument

Refer to the following argument and accompanying prompts to help you when writing your own argument.

Hint at or state your main claim in the title.

Hook the reader with a strong opening statement then explain your claim.

Organize each reason in a separate paragraph.

Support each reason with relevant evidence.

Use transition words, phrases, and clauses to link ideas and paragraphs.

Restate your claim and leave the reader with something to think about.

Always use formal language when writing an argument, as though you are writing to someone you don't know.

Grow Your Own Food!

Growing your own fruit and vegetables can harvest many rewards. I believe that every family, no matter their circumstances, should have a chance at growing their own food.

Firstly, it is important to remember that homegrown food is great for the environment. Food that is transported to a supermarket relies on transport, such as planes, ships, trucks, and cars. This adds to air pollution, which is a big threat to our planet and our health. Home-grown food doesn't need to be transported.

In addition, growing your own food is a great way to save money, as you don't need to buy the fruit and vegetables that you are growing at home. The average American household spends over $1000 per month at the grocery store. Reducing this cost means a big benefit for families and their spending.

Some people will argue that not everyone can grow their own food, because they don't have a garden. However, even if you live in an apartment you can still grow many fruits, vegetables, and herbs in pots, such as green beans, tomatoes, chives, and basil. Some neighborhoods may also have a community garden that you can join.

In conclusion, I strongly believe that growing your own food can be a rewarding pastime with multiple benefits. And even better—you get to eat the fruits of your labors!

Note for student: Read your argument aloud afterward to check your grammar, punctuation, and spelling.

Now write your own argument using the notes you have prepared from pages 46-47. You may want to use additional paper to complete your argument.

Title: ....

Writing Poetry

Poetry uses words in imaginative ways to paint pictures, describe feelings and ideas, or explore emotions. There are many tools that poets can use in their writing. Here are some examples.

Alliteration	Repeating the same sound at the beginning of words:	The haunted house stood high on the hill.
Hyperbole	Using exaggeration for humor or to emphasize a point:	Spaghetti strands a mile long slipped off the plate!
Imagery	Creating a picture by describing something:	The lone eagle soared over the gray mountains.
Line breaks	Writing in short lines to slow the reader:	Inch by inch, Step by step, He crept closer.
Oxymoron	Putting words together with opposite meanings:	The quiet noise woke the mouse.
Personification	Giving human characteristics to something that is not human:	The autumn wind whispered through the trees.
Repetition	Repeating the same word for effect:	On a cold wet night, In the cold wet winter, A cold wet cat walked by.

For each of these examples, check ✔ which one the poet has used.

1. The leaves danced in the wind,
   Doing cartwheels and somersaults.
   — personification ○ repetition ○ oxymoron ○

2. Peter Piper picked a peck of pickled peppers.
   A peck of pickled peppers Peter Piper picked.
   — imagery ○ alliteration ○ line breaks ○

3. She spoke in a loud whisper,
   A dim light shone from her torch.
   — repetition ○ oxymoron ○ personification ○

Note for student: Look at different examples of poetry and identify the tools that poets have used to communicate their ideas, feelings, and emotions.

Similes and Metaphors

Similes and metaphors are other tools poets can use to help make descriptions more interesting and imaginative. They are used to make comparisons to something a reader may already be familiar with.

> Similes use **as** or **like** to make a comparison, whereas a metaphor compares two things without using **as** or **like**.

Look at the photograph below.
Check ✔ the similes that would best describe the Moon.

| like a watchful eye ○ | like a space rocket ○ | like a shiny pearl ○ |
| as big as a house ○ | as pale as winter ○ | as black as night ○ |

Check ✔ the metaphors that would best describe the calm sea.

| a blue blanket ○ | an angry beast ○ | a crash of thunder ○ |
| a giant's fists ○ | a glittering treasure ○ | a polished mirror ○ |

Write your own poem to describe the pictured scene. Include some of the similes and metaphors you have checked above, or create your own. You may also want to use some of the poetry tools from the opposite page.

....
....
....
....
....
....
....

Note for student: By making interesting and unusual comparisons, a writer can create engaging descriptions to attract the reader.

Personification

In this poem, the poet uses personification to give human/physical characteristics to something that is not human—the sun. Read the poem, then answer the questions.

The Voyage of the Sun

Gallant captain rises in the East,
His gold-spun **linen** on full show,
A journey started once again,
His beaming smile set all aglow.

Oars spilling warmth with certain strokes
The sky his map to punctual end.
Through storms of cloud and angry gale
Towards the West and then descend.

His fond farewell waves orange hues,
Sinking slowly into lands of night,
Where fell beasts roam and **specters** call.
Yet none may dim his lantern light.

His voyage may be long and fraught,
But **lodestone** sure, the East is found.
The captain throws aloft his mast,
His shining voyage starts around.

linen: (n.)
a common type of fabric in the ancient world

specter: (n.)
a ghost or apparition

lodestone: (n.)
a magnetic rock used to navigate, before the invention of the compass

Note for student: The poem is inspired by the Ancient Egyptian's belief that the sun was a sailboat. It traveled through the sky by day, then through the underworld at night.

1. Who or what is the sun being compared to?

   ....

2. What natural cycle/event is the poet describing in this poem?

   ....

3. Do you think the poem is set in modern-day times? Explain your answer.

   ....

   ....

4. In stanza 3, what does the poet imagine happens once night falls?

   ....

   ....

5. What effect does the poet's use of personification have on *you* as the reader?

   ....

   ....

6. Choose from one of the poem titles below. Write an opening verse using personification to give human characteristics to the object you are describing.

   A gentle breeze   A rushing river   A stormy sky

   ....

   ....

   ....

   ....

53

Poem Structure

In "What is Pink?", the poet explores the colors of nature using a question-and-answer structure.

What is Pink?

What is pink? A rose is pink ← Each question is answered with a concrete noun.
By the fountain's brink. ← The follow-up sentence gives further description.
What is red? A poppy's red
In its barley bed.
What is blue? The sky is blue
Where the clouds float through.
What is white? A swan is white
Sailing in the light.
What is yellow? Pears are yellow,
Rich and ripe and mellow.
What is green? The grass is green,
With small flowers between.
What is violet? Clouds are violet
In the summer twilight.
What is orange? Why, an orange,
Just an orange!

By Christina Rossetti

A concrete noun is something physical you can experience through your senses, such as: sand, sea, wind, trees, grass, house, table, school, sidewalk, etc.

Use your own color choice and ideas to complete this color poem.

What is .... ? .... ← a concrete noun

.... ← a description

What is .... ? ....

....

What is .... ? ....

....

Try to use rhyming words to link each pair of verses.

Note for student: The structure of a poem refers to the way that the poet has organized their text for the reader. This might include line spacing, line length, and the size of stanzas.

In this poem, the same poet uses a question-and-answer structure for dramatic effect.

What Are Heavy?

What are heavy? Sea-sand and sorrow;
What are brief? Today and tomorrow;
What are frail? Spring blossom and youth;
What are deep? The ocean and truth.

By Christina Rossetti

The poet answers her questions using concrete and abstract nouns.

> An abstract noun is an idea, emotion, or concept that you can't physically experience through your senses, such as: sorrow, truth, love, anger, peace, today, tomorrow, etc.

Complete this poem by answering each question using a concrete and an abstract noun. If you wish, you can copy the rhyme scheme from the poem above.

What are bright? .... and ....

What are strong? .... and ....

What are cold? .... and ....

What are loud? .... and ....

What are sweet? .... and ....

What are calming? .... and ....

Story Structure

Most stories follow the same structure, which can be broken down into five parts.

1. Exposition
This is the start of the story that describes the characters, setting, and the main conflict.
- Characters: the people, or creatures, who will appear in the story.
- Setting: when and where the story will take place.
- Conflict: the main problem to be solved, or obstacle to be overcome.

2. Rising action
This section builds tension and excitement. It describes the struggle of the main character as he/she attempts to tackle and overcome the problem in the story (the conflict).

3. Climax
This is the big turning point when the conflict is resolved, either by solving the problem, or overcoming the obstacle.

4. Falling action
This is the slowing down part of the story that deals with the events after the climax of the story. It describes how the major parts of the story are resolved. This leads the reader toward the resolution.

5. Resolution
This is the end of the story and describes how the main character, or the situation, has changed.

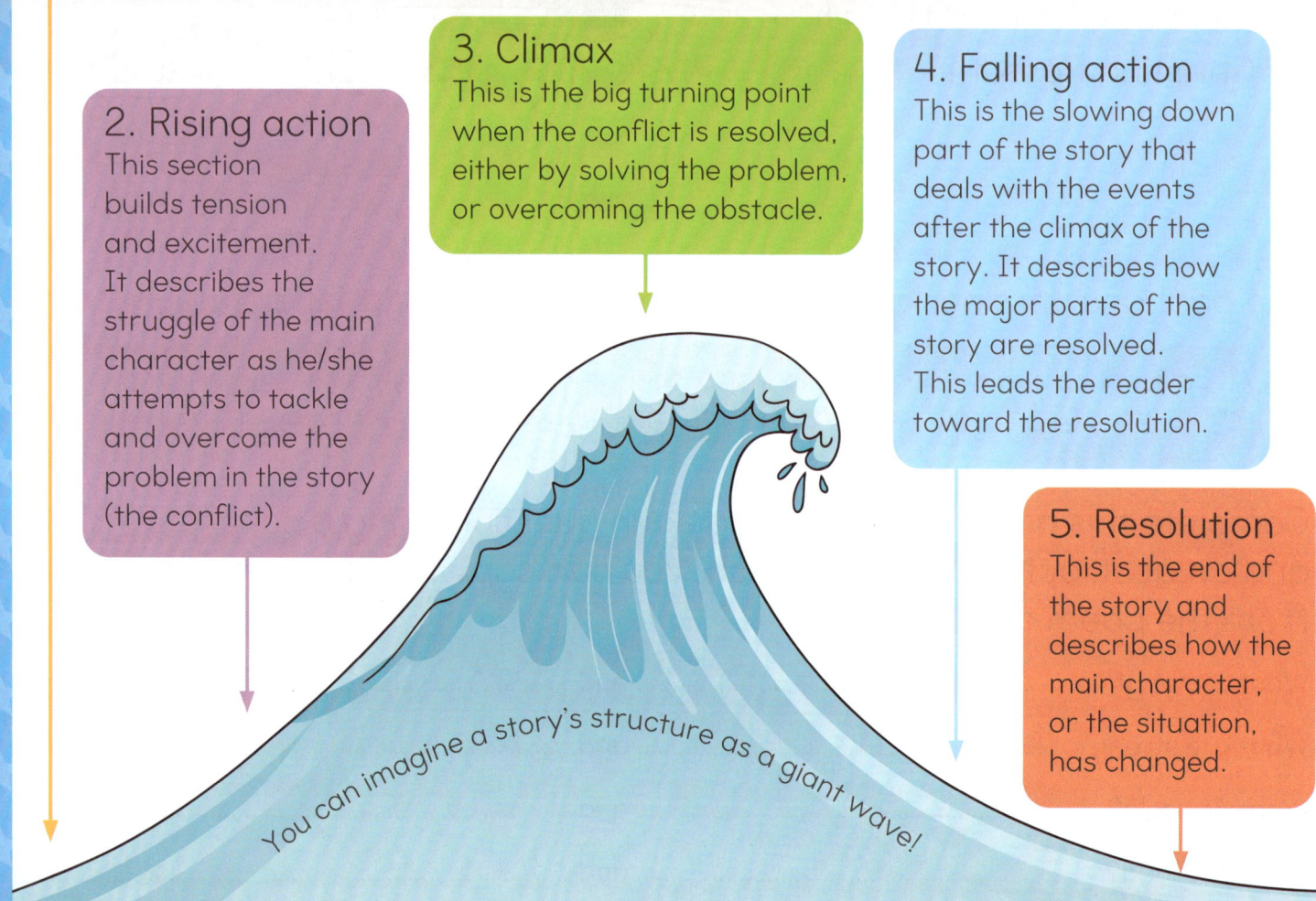

You can imagine a story's structure as a giant wave!

When you write a story, it is important to have a good structure. This will ensure that your readers understand what is happening in your story and be entertained by it.

Note for student: Understanding the basic structure of a story can help you when planning and writing your own stories.

Revisit the story, *Raven Steals the Light* (see pages 20–21). Copy the following notes into the graphic organizer below to show the progression and structure of the story.

- Raven loses the light as a result of a chase.
- Raven puts his plan into action to steal the light.
- Raven steals the light from the box.
- Light is restored to the world, and the daughter marries.

3. Climax
....
....
....

2. Rising action
....
....
....

4. Falling action
....
....
....

1. Exposition
Characters:
Raven, Sky Father, Daughter
Setting:
A world of darkness.
Conflict:
Sky Father has the light in a box.

5. Resolution
....
....
....

Who Tells the Story

A story can be written from different points of view.

Third person narration is when the story is told by someone who is not in the story. Usually, this is a narrator who is describing what is happening to the characters in the story.

First person narration is when the story is told by a character who is in the story, using pronouns such as: **I**, **me**, **my**, **mine**, **myself**, **we**, **us**, and **our**.

Rewrite this paragraph by changing it from third person narration to first person narration.

Colt Phoenix wrestled with the controls of his spacecraft. Alarm bells were ringing and warning lights flashing. He knew that things were going from bad to worse. The engine was losing power and soon his thrusters would cease to work. Behind him, the alien mothership was closing in. Colt turned his ship into a steep dive toward the nearby asteroids. He was the best pilot in the academy but was he good enough to make it through alive? He told himself, I can do it!

I wrestled with the controls of my spacecraft. Alarm bells were ringing and warning lights flashing.

Note for student: First person narration can make action feel more dramatic, and helps us to empathize with the main character more.

Story Plot

The plot of a story is the sequence of events that leads the reader from the beginning to the end of the story. A good plot introduces a **conflict** for the protagonist to overcome, and works toward a **resolution** to bring the story to a satisfying conclusion.

Choose a story starter, and write about how you would develop the plot by introducing conflict (a problem) and what the resolution (conclusion) might be.

Plot idea: rags to riches

Aladdin had discovered an old lamp buried in the sand. He wondered if the lamp might have a genie inside who would grant him his wishes. Aladdin had always wanted to be rich...

Plot idea: something goes missing

Izzy was late for school again and Mom was angry. Today was science demonstration day and the special model Izzy had been working on all summer was nowhere to be found...

....
....
....
....
....
....

Note for student: A good story should present a problem, or obstacle, for the main character. This encourages the reader to empathize with and support the character.

Writing a Scene

The following is an excerpt of a playscript adapted from Chapter 2 of *Treasure Island* by Robert Louis Stevenson.

Setting: *The Admiral Benbow Inn*
Characters: The Captain (Billy Bones), Jim (the innkeeper's son), Black Dog (a mysterious pirate)

(Jim is laying out a table for breakfast. Black Dog enters.)
Jim: *(to the audience)* I'd never set eyes on this one before. He was skinny and pale, missing two fingers of the left hand.
Black Dog *(snappily)* : Hey, sonny.
Jim *(startles)* : Yes, sir.
Black Dog: Come nearer.
(Jim nervously takes a step closer.)
Black Dog: Is this here table for my mate, Billy Bones?
Jim *(shakes his head)* : I don't know a Billy Bones. This is for the Captain.
Black Dog *(leers)* : Ah, yes. He'd call himself the Captain. A cut on one cheek, yes?
Jim: He's not here. He's out walking.
(Black Dog pulls out a chair and sits down.)
Black Dog: I'll wait then. Go get me a cup of rum.
(Jim is about to leave when the Captain enters.)
Black Dog: Well, well. If it ain't the Captain.
(The Captain stands frozen.)
Black Dog: What's the matter? Look like you seen a ghost. Come, Bill. You know me, your old shipmate.
The Captain *(gasping)* : Black Dog. How…?
(Jim backs into a corner.)
Black Dog: You knows what I want and I come to collect.
The Captain: No, and that's an end to it.
(Black Dog leaps up. Both pirates draw their cutlasses and fight. Black Dog is wounded and flees.)
The Captain *(exhausted)* : Jim, my lad. Some rum to settle me nerves.
Jim: Who was he?
The Captain: The ghost of me past.

Note for student: This scene features the same location as the excerpt on pages 16–17, and adds a new character, and further plot developments.

Now write your own version of this scene as a narrative piece of writing with paragraphs, quotation marks, and description as it might appear in a storybook. You may want to use additional paper to complete your story scene.

Decide if you will use first or third person narration.

Provide an opening that will hook your reader.

Use direct and indirect characterization to add interest to your characters.

Organize your scene into paragraphs.

Use quotation marks to indicate direct speech.

Decimals and Fractions

Student Notes

The activities in this section will help you learn how to:

- Convert to decimal numbers, and multiply and divide decimals by powers of ten.

- Multiply and divide fractions, and multiply a fraction by another fraction.

- Calculate ratios, rates, and percentages.

You may choose to work on the activities independently, or you may want help from a parent or other adult at the start of an activity.

Contents

Exponents	64
Multi-Digit Division	66
Multiply Decimals by Powers of Ten	68
Divide Decimals by Powers of Ten	69
Decimal Multiplication	70
Dividing Decimals	72
Fractions and Division	74
Multiply the Quick Way	76
Multiply a Fraction by a Fraction	78
Rectangles with Fractional Sides	80
Divide a Fraction by a Whole Number	82
Divide a Whole Number by a Fraction	84
Understanding Ratio	86
Ratio Tables	87
Ratio Problems	88
Equivalent Ratios	89
Understanding Rate	90
Percentages	92
Answers	125

Exponents

What is an **exponent**?
An exponent is also known as a "power." It tells us how many times we multiply a base number by itself.

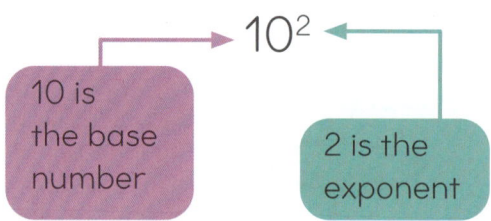
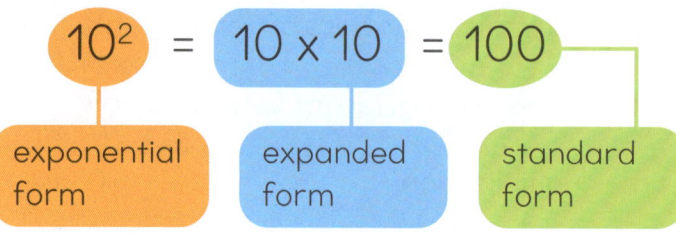

When referring to 10^2 we can say, "10 to the power of 2," or "10 squared."

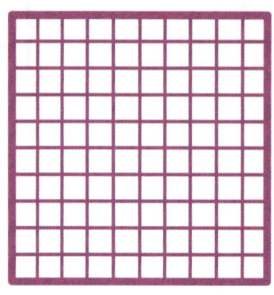

$10^2 = 100$

When we multiply a whole number by itself the product is called a "square number."

$1 \times 1 = 1$, $2 \times 2 = 4$, $3 \times 3 = 9$, $4 \times 4 = 16$, $5 \times 5 = 25$, and so on. The products 1, 4, 9, 16, and 25 are square numbers.

$10^3 = 10 \times 10 \times 10$
$ = 100 \times 10$
$ = 1{,}000$

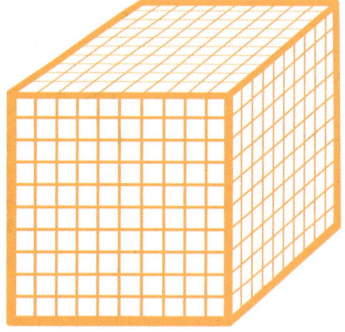

For 10^3 we say, "10 to the power of 3," or "10 cubed" because this number looks like a cube.

$10^3 = 1{,}000$

The products of these multiplications are cube numbers:
$1 \times 1 \times 1 = 1$, $2 \times 2 \times 2 = 8$, $3 \times 3 \times 3 = 27$, $4 \times 4 \times 4 = 64$, $5 \times 5 \times 5 = 125$.

1 x 1 x 1   2 x 2 x 2   3 x 3 x 3

Note for student: It is a common mistake to think that $10^2 = 10 \times 2$. You need to remember that $10^2 = 10 \times 10$.

Figure out the products. Can you see a pattern forming?

10^1 = 10

10^2 = 10 × 10 = ...

10^3 = 10 × 10 × 10

   = 100 × 10 = ...

10^4 = 10 × 10 × 10 × 10

   = ... × 10 = ...

10^5 = 10 × 10 × 10 × 10 × 10

   = ... × 10 = ...

10^6 = 10 × 10 × 10 × 10 × 10 × 10

   = ... × 10 = ...

Put in commas to separate thousands by starting from the last digit in the number and counting backward in threes.

1 2	1 2 3	1 2 3 4	1 2 3 4 5	1 2 3 4 5 6
10^2 = 100	10^3 = 1,000	10^4 = 10,000	10^5 = 100,000	10^6 = 1,000,000
2 zeros	☐ zeros	☐ zeros	☐ zeros	☐ zeros

Write the expanded form then figure out the product.

10^7 = 10 × 10 × 10 × 10 × 10 × 10 × 10 = ...

10^8 = ...

10^9 = ...

10^{10} = ...

Multi-Digit Division

Suppose you wanted to find out the answer to this problem: **If you saved $35 per month, how long would it take you to buy a guitar that costs $735?** You could write this problem as **735 ÷ 35** and use an area model to find the answer.

Step 1: Figure out some useful multiples of the divisor.
35 × 2 = 70
35 × 10 = 350
35 × 20 = 700

Step 2: After 10 months you have saved $350 and after 20 months $700.

Step 3: You need to save for one more month.

Step 4: In total, you need to save for 21 months to buy the guitar.

×	10	10	1
35	350	350	35

```
  735     385     35
- 350   - 350   - 35
  ___     ___    ___
  385      35     0
```

If **484 stickers are shared equally between 22 children, how many stickers would each child get?** This problem could be written as **484 ÷ 22**. Complete the area model.

Useful multiples:
22 × 2 = ...
22 × 10 = ...
22 × 20 = ...

×	20	2
22	440	

```
   484
 - 440    -
  ____     ____
    44
```

Answer: Each child gets  stickers.

Note for student: You can use different factors with area models though you will find it easier to subtract from the total in groups of ten.

630 children are going to school by minibus. If each minibus can take 15 passengers, how many minibuses will be needed?

This problem could be written as: ☐ ÷ ☐.

Complete the area model.

Useful multiples:
15 × 2 = ...
15 × 10 = ...
15 × 20 = ...
15 × 40 = ...

×	40	2
15	600	

6 3 0
−   −
_____   _____

....

Answer: ☐ minibuses will be needed.

552 people are sitting in a movie theater in equal rows of 24 people. How many rows of people are there?

This problem could be written as: ☐ ÷ ☐.

Complete the area model.

Useful multiples:
24 × 2 = ...
24 × 10 = ...
24 × 20 = ...

×	20	2	1
24	480		

5 5 2
−   −   −
_____   _____   _____

....

Answer: There are ☐ rows of people.

67

Multiply Decimals by Powers of Ten

Placing zeros at the end of the number doesn't work when we multiply decimals. We need to move the decimal point to the right to increase the value of the number.

✗ 4.2 x 10 = 4.20 is wrong because the number is still the same value

✓ 4.2 x 10 = 42 is correct because 42 is 10 times greater than 4.2

The arrows below show you the decimal moves one place to the right when we multiply by 10 and two places to the right when we multiply by 100.

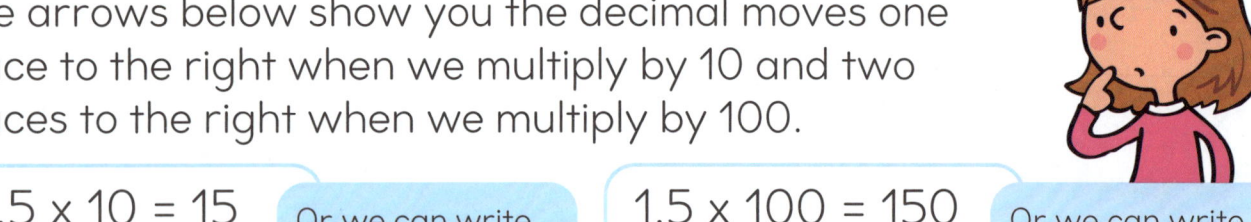

1.5 x 10 = 15
1.5

Or we can write 15.0 as a decimal number.

1.5 x 100 = 150
1.50

Or we can write 150.0 as a decimal number.

Circle the correct products for these decimal multiplication problems.

1. 2.3 x 10 = 230 or 23
2. 0.5 x 10 = 50 or 5
3. 17.5 x 10 = 175 or 1,750
4. 5.6 x 100 = 560 or 56
5. 1.8 x 100 = 1,800 or 180
6. 42.15 x 100 = 4,215 or 42,150

If you are unsure of your answer, there is a quick way of checking. Look at the first problem as an example.

Step 1: Find the nearest whole number to the decimal. The nearest whole number to 2.3 is 2.

Step 2: Multiply 2 by 10. The answer is 20. So a reasonable answer will be close to this number.

Step 3: Choose between 230 or 23. The answer must be 23!

Note for student: This activity will help you understand that when we move a decimal point to the right we are increasing the value of the number.

Divide Decimals by Powers of Ten

Deleting zeros at the end of the number doesn't work when we divide decimals. We need to move the decimal point to the left to decrease the value of the number.

✗ 4.20 ÷ 10 = 4.2 is wrong because the number is still the same value

✓ 4.20 ÷ 10 = 0.42 is correct because 0.42 is 10 times less than 4.20

The arrows below show you the decimal moves one place to the left when we divide by 10 and two places to the left when we divide by 100.

15.0 ÷ 10 = 1.50
1 5 . 0

Or we can write 1.5

15.0 ÷ 100 = 0.15
1 5 . 0

We write 0.15 with zero as a placeholder

Circle the correct quotients for these decimal division problems.

1. 9.9 ÷ 10   = 0.99   or   99

2. 17.3 ÷ 10   = 173   or   1.73

3. 48.6 ÷ 10   = 486   or   4.86

4. 384.0 ÷ 100 = 3.84   or   38.4

5. 52.0 ÷ 100   = 5.20   or   0.52

6. 499.0 ÷ 100 = 4.99   or   49.90

If you are unsure of your answer, there is a quick way of checking. Look at the first problem as an example.

Step 1: Find the nearest whole number to the decimal. The nearest whole number is 10.

Step 2: Divide 10 by 10. The answer is 1. So a reasonable answer will be close to 1.

Step 3: Choose between 0.99 and 99. The answer must be 0.99!

Note for student: This activity will help you understand that when we move a decimal point to the left we are decreasing the value of the number.

Decimal Multiplication

Multiplying decimals is like whole number multiplication except that when you have your product, you then have to write the decimal in the correct place.

Follow these steps:

Step 1: Multiply in the normal way, ignoring the decimals.

Step 2: Count the total number of decimal places after the decimal point in both factors.

Step 3: Go to your answer and count back from the right the total number of places, then write the decimal point.

Step 4: Check that your product is reasonable.

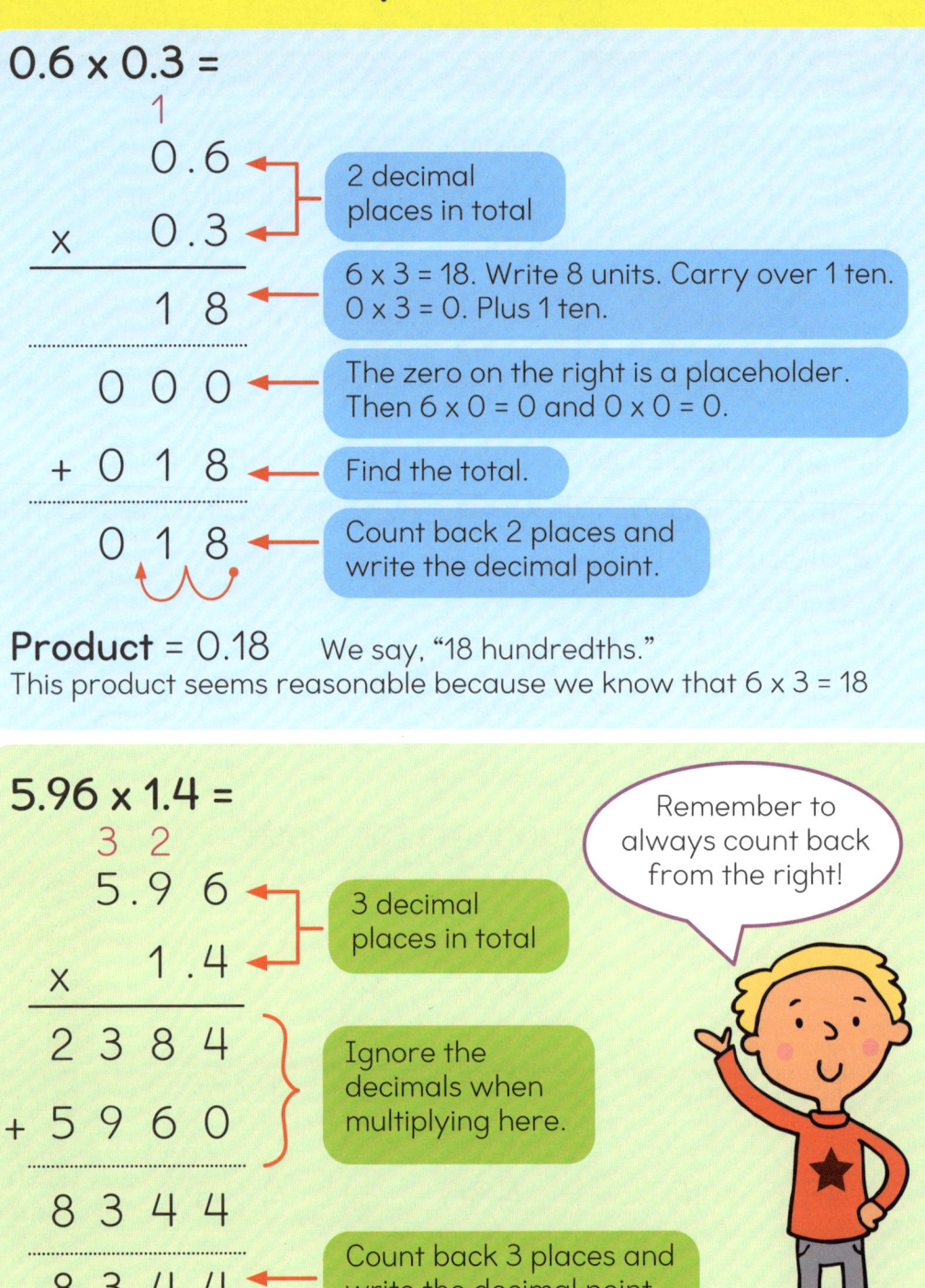

0.6 × 0.3 =

```
      1
      0.6     ← 2 decimal places in total
  ×   0.3     ←
    ─────
      1 8     ← 6 × 3 = 18. Write 8 units. Carry over 1 ten.
                 0 × 3 = 0. Plus 1 ten.
    0 0 0     ← The zero on the right is a placeholder.
                 Then 6 × 0 = 0 and 0 × 0 = 0.
  + 0 1 8     ← Find the total.
    ─────
    0 1 8     ← Count back 2 places and write the decimal point.
```

Product = 0.18   We say, "18 hundredths."
This product seems reasonable because we know that 6 × 3 = 18

5.96 × 1.4 =

```
    3 2
    5.9 6     ← 3 decimal places in total
  ×   1.4     ←
    ─────
    2 3 8 4   ⎫ Ignore the
  + 5 9 6 0   ⎭ decimals when multiplying here.
    ───────
    8 3 4 4
    ───────
    8.3 4 4   ← Count back 3 places and write the decimal point.
```

Product = 8.344
We say, "Eight and three hundred forty-four thousandths."
This product seems reasonable if we round the factors to 6 × 1.5 (or 6 × 1½) = 9

× 6 = 1.5 + 1.5 + 1.5 + 1.5 + 1.5 + 1.5 = 9

Remember to always count back from the right!

Note for student: Try to think of different ways to check the products by rounding and/or visualizing the factors.

Here are some more decimal multiplication problems.

8.96 x 4 =

```
   8 . 9 6   ← 2 decimal places
 x       4   ← 4 is a whole number so multiply as you would normally do.
 ─────────
```

Product = ☐

Round the 8.96 to a whole factor to check if your product is reasonable.

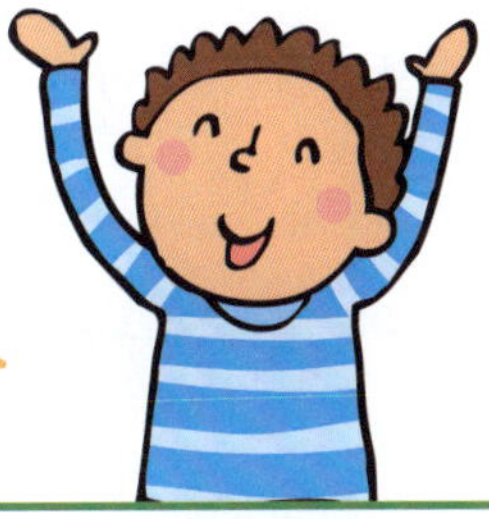

1.01 x 0.5 =

```
   1 . 0 1   ← 3 decimal places in total
 x   0 . 5   ←
 ─────────
         
 +       
 ─────────
```

If you round the factors, this is like 1 x 0.5 (or 0.5 x 1) = 0.5 so your product will be close to 0.5!

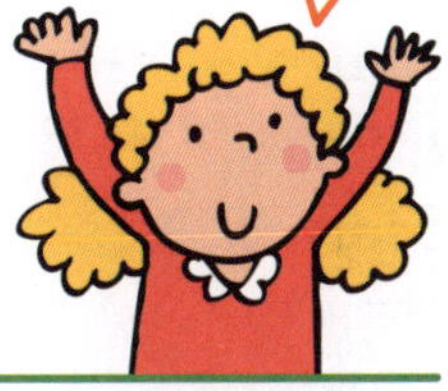

Product = ☐

6.95 x 5.1 =

```
   6 . 9 5
 x   5 . 1
 ─────────

 +
 ─────────
```

Round the factors to check if your product is reasonable.

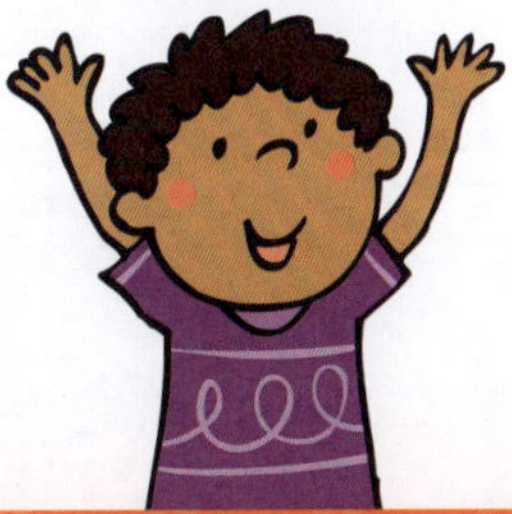

Product = ☐

17.45 x 3.2 =

```
   17 . 4 5
 x    3 . 2
 ──────────

 +
 ──────────
```

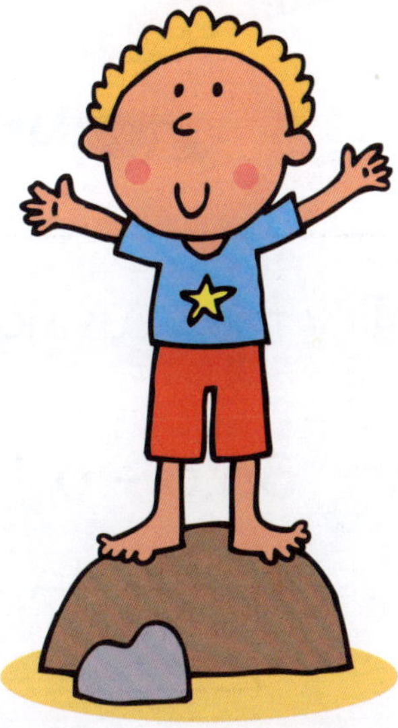

Product = ☐

71

Dividing Decimals

If your divisor is a whole number, dividing decimals is like whole number division. All you have to do is to write the decimal in your quotient directly above the decimal in the dividend.

Follow these steps:

Step 1: Check the divisor. If this is a whole number, write the decimal on the answer line directly above the decimal in the dividend.

Step 2: Divide in the usual way.

Step 3: Check that your quotient is reasonable.

Remember the terms: divisor | dividend / quotient

$97.5 \div 3 =$

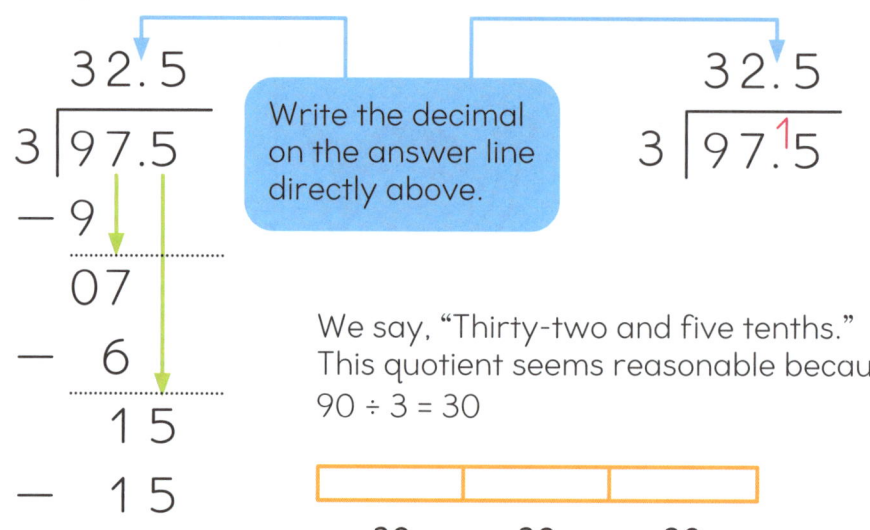

Long division:

```
    32.5
3 ) 97.5
   -9
    07
   - 6
     15
   - 15
      0
```

Write the decimal on the answer line directly above.

Short division:

```
   32.5
3 ) 97.¹5
```

We say, "Thirty-two and five tenths." This quotient seems reasonable because $90 \div 3 = 30$

| 30 | 30 | 30 |

Try these using short division.

$36.6 \div 6 =$

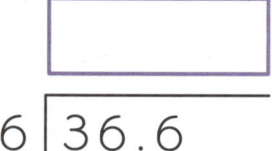

6) 36.6

$28.44 \div 4 =$

4) 28.44

$837.6 \div 2 =$

2) 837.6

Note for student: You can apply different strategies to solve these division problems. This activity uses written methods combined with reasoning skills and modeling.

If your divisor is a decimal number then you will need to make it a whole number by moving the decimal point. Then, whatever you do to the divisor you do to the dividend.

Follow these steps:

Step 1: Multiply the decimal divisor by a power of 10 to make a whole number, and move the decimal point to the right.

Step 2: Whatever you do to the divisor, you have to do the same to the dividend.

Step 3: Divide in the usual way.

Step 4: Check that your quotient is reasonable.

$14.4 \div 1.2 = 14.4 \div 1.2 = 144 \div 12$

×10   ×10

```
      12.
  12 | 144.
     − 12
       ———
        24
      − 24
       ———
         0
```

How many groups of 12 are in 144? You can do this division mentally if you know your times tables.

Try these using short division.

$98.8 \div 0.4 =$

$98.8 \div 0.4$

×10   ×10

$= 988 \div 4$

```
  ▭
4 | 988.
```

Check that your quotient is reasonable. Remember 1,000 ÷ 4 = 250. Is your answer close to this?

$25.5 \div 0.5 =$

$25.5 \div 0.5$

×10   ×10

$= 255 \div 5$

```
  ▭
5 | 255.
```

Fractions and Division

Fractions and division are related. The fraction $\frac{1}{2}$ means 1 whole divided by 2.

We can write: $\frac{1}{2}$ or $1 \div 2$ or $2\overline{)1}$

Rewrite these word problems as fractions and divide to find the answers or quotients.

Example: Three friends wash their neighbors' cars. They earn 36 dollars in total which they share equally. Write a fraction that shows how much money they each earn.

We can write this as: $36 \div 3$ or $3\overline{)36}$

or as a fraction: $\frac{36}{3}$ ← Total money they earn / Shared by 3 friends

$\frac{36}{3} = \boxed{}$ They each earn $\boxed{}$ dollars.

Remember the terms:

numerator and dividend ⟶ $\frac{20}{5} = 4$ ← answer or quotient
denominator and divisor ⟶

Try these yourself.

1. Alex has 24 party favors that he wants to share equally into 6 party bags. How many party favors go into each bag?

$\frac{\boxed{}}{6} = \boxed{}$ party favors in each bag.

2. Amir is planting flower bulbs. He has 64 bulbs in total and 8 plant pots. If he divides the bulbs equally between the pots, how many bulbs go in each pot?

$\frac{64}{\boxed{}} = \boxed{}$ bulbs in each pot.

Note for student: This activity demonstrates how fractions and division (which is often called "sharing" in word problems) are related.

If there is a remainder in the quotient, you can convert this to a fraction.

$\frac{7}{2} = 3 \text{ r } 1 = 3\frac{1}{2}$ ← The remainder is $\frac{1}{2}$ because this is $1 \div 2$.

$\frac{37}{6} = 6 \text{ r } 1 = 6\frac{1}{6}$ ← The remainder is $\frac{1}{6}$ because this is $1 \div 6$.

Try these. They have remainders that you need to convert to fractions.

3. Ruby and Reggie are together writing a 19-page drama script. If they share the writing, how many pages do they each have to write?

They each have to write $\frac{19}{\Box} = \Box \frac{\Box}{\Box}$ pages.

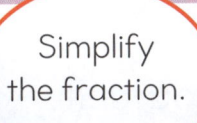
Simplify the fraction.

4. A teacher has 28 sheets of colored paper that she wants to share equally with 8 children. How many sheets of colored paper do they each get?

They each get $\frac{\Box}{8} = \Box \frac{\Box}{\Box} = \Box \frac{\Box}{\Box}$ sheets.

75

Multiply the Quick Way

Here is a quicker method you can use to multiply fractions. For example:

$3 \times \dfrac{2}{3}$ = **Step 1:** $\dfrac{3}{1}$ **×** **Step 2:** $\dfrac{2}{3}$ = **Step 3:** $\dfrac{6}{3} = 2$

Step 1:
Take the first factor (the whole number) and turn it into a fraction with 3 as the numerator and 1 as the denominator.

Step 2:
Multiply the numerator by the numerator, and the denominator by the denominator.

Step 3:
Simplify the fraction if you can.

Notice our product (which is the answer 2) is less than the first factor we started with (3) because we multiplied by another factor that was less than 1 (it was $\dfrac{2}{3}$).

Try these yourself.

1. $(4) \times \dfrac{3}{5} = \dfrac{\square}{1} \times \dfrac{3}{5} = \dfrac{\square}{\square} = \square \dfrac{\square}{\square}$

Write the whole number as a fraction with 1 as the denominator.

Note for student: Remember, a whole number always has 1 as its denominator.

2. $5 \times \dfrac{5}{6} = \dfrac{\boxed{}}{1} \times \dfrac{5}{6} = \dfrac{\boxed{}}{\boxed{}} = \boxed{}\dfrac{\boxed{}}{\boxed{}}$

3. $3 \times \dfrac{3}{4} = \dfrac{\boxed{}}{1} \times \dfrac{3}{4} = \dfrac{\boxed{}}{\boxed{}} = \boxed{}\dfrac{\boxed{}}{\boxed{}}$

4. $6 \times \dfrac{5}{8} = \dfrac{\boxed{}}{1} \times \dfrac{5}{8} = \dfrac{\boxed{}}{\boxed{}} = \boxed{}\dfrac{\boxed{}}{\boxed{}} = \boxed{}\dfrac{\boxed{}}{\boxed{}}$

5. $7 \times \dfrac{3}{10} = \dfrac{\boxed{}}{1} \times \dfrac{3}{10} = \dfrac{\boxed{}}{\boxed{}} = \boxed{}\dfrac{\boxed{}}{\boxed{}}$

6. $8 \times \dfrac{7}{8} = \dfrac{\boxed{}}{1} \times \dfrac{7}{8} = \dfrac{\boxed{}}{\boxed{}} = \boxed{}$

7. $9 \times \dfrac{5}{12} = \dfrac{\boxed{}}{1} \times \dfrac{5}{12} = \dfrac{\boxed{}}{\boxed{}} = \boxed{}\dfrac{\boxed{}}{\boxed{}} = \boxed{}\dfrac{\boxed{}}{\boxed{}}$

77

Multiply a Fraction by a Fraction

If I have $\frac{1}{2}$ a candy bar and my 2 friends share it with me, we each have $\frac{1}{3}$ of $\frac{1}{2}$. How much is that?

We can solve this problem by using a model.

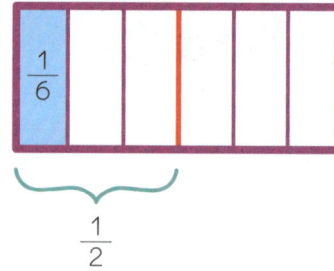

$\frac{1}{3}$ of $\frac{1}{2} = \frac{1}{6}$

Or we can write an equation:

$\frac{1}{3} \times \frac{1}{2}$

Read the multiplication sign as "of."

When multiplying a fraction by a fraction there is only one rule to remember: work straight across.

Multiply

$\frac{1}{3} \times \frac{1}{2} = \frac{1}{6}$

Check the math! Our equation and our model both give us the same answer.

Use the model and write an equation to solve these problems.

1. A puppy ate $\frac{1}{3}$ of $\frac{1}{4}$ of a bowl of dog food. How much did the puppy eat?

$\frac{1}{3} \times \frac{1}{4} = \boxed{}$

Note for student: Being able to draw models to represent problems is a valuable math skill. You can use these models to check written methods.

2. Jorge cut some banana bread into fourths and he ate $\frac{1}{2}$ of $\frac{1}{4}$. How much did he eat?

$\frac{1}{2} \times \frac{1}{4} = \boxed{\phantom{\frac{a}{b}}}$

3. A rabbit ate $\frac{2}{3}$ of $\frac{1}{4}$ of a carrot. How much is that?

$\frac{2}{3} \times \frac{1}{4} = \boxed{\phantom{\frac{a}{b}}} = \boxed{\phantom{\frac{a}{b}}}$

4. I spent $\frac{3}{5}$ of $\frac{1}{2}$ of my allowance. How much is that?

$\frac{3}{5} \times \frac{1}{2} = \boxed{\phantom{\frac{a}{b}}}$

Rectangles with Fractional Sides

The rectangle below has fractional sides. This means the sides are fractions, not whole numbers.

To find the area of this rectangle, we use the formula:

Area = Length x Width ⟶ Area = $\frac{3}{4}$ x $\frac{2}{3}$

We multiply straight across, then simplify the answer.

Multiply　　　　**Simplify**

$\frac{3}{4}$ x $\frac{2}{3}$ = $\frac{6}{12}$ = $\frac{1}{2}$　　Divide both numbers by 6 to simplify.

Answer: Area = $\frac{1}{2}$ square units

We can draw an area model to check if our math is correct.

Step 1: Draw a rectangle and divide it into 4 quarters vertically.

Step 2: Divide the rectangle into 3 thirds horizontally.

Step 3: Color $\frac{3}{4}$ of the rectangle red.

Step 4: Color $\frac{2}{3}$ of the rectangle green.

Step 5: Count the number of parts that overlap. This is the numerator.

Step 6: Count the total number of parts in the rectangle. This is the denominator.

 $\frac{2}{3}$ is green　　 $\frac{3}{4}$ is red

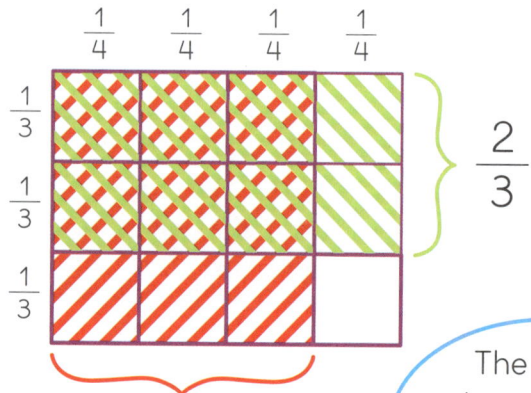

$\frac{6}{12}$ = $\frac{1}{2}$

 Count the parts that overlap.

Count the total number of parts in the rectangle.

The model shows us that our equation is correct.

Note for student: The area model helps you to visualize what fractions look like in reality.

1. What is the area of a rectangle with fractional sides of $\frac{4}{5}$ x $\frac{3}{4}$ units?

Multiply   Simplify

$\frac{4}{5}$ x $\frac{3}{4}$ = ▭ = ▭   Answer: Area = ▭ square units

Now use the model and color $\frac{4}{5}$ x $\frac{3}{4}$ to show that your equation (above) is correct.

▭ = ▭

Count the parts that overlap.

Count the total number of parts in the rectangle.

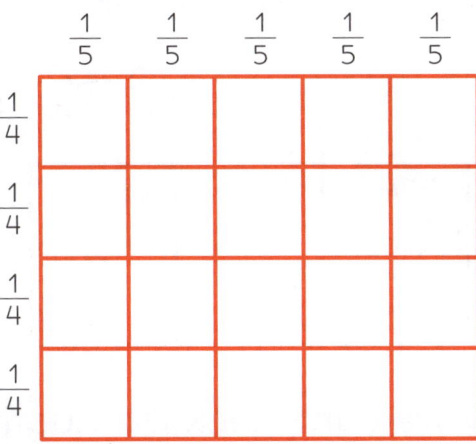

---

2. What is the area of a rectangle with fractional sides of $\frac{5}{6}$ x $\frac{1}{2}$ units?

Multiply

$\frac{5}{6}$ x $\frac{1}{2}$ = ▭   Answer: Area = ▭ square units

Now use the model and color $\frac{5}{6}$ x $\frac{1}{2}$ to show that your equation (above) is correct.

▭

Count the parts that overlap.

Count the total number of parts in the rectangle.

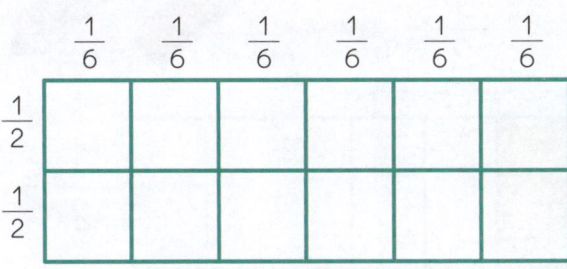

Does the model show your equation is correct?

81

Divide a Fraction by a Whole Number

Read the problems and use the models to find the quotients.

1. A teacher shares $\frac{1}{3}$ of a sheet of stickers equally among 4 children. What fraction of the whole sheet of stickers does each child get? $\frac{1}{3} \div 4$

We can use a model to solve this problem. Draw a rectangle and divide it into thirds. Then take one third and divide it into four sections.

$\frac{1}{3} \div 4 = \frac{1}{12}$

Each child gets $\boxed{}$ of the whole sheet of stickers.

Now we can check the quotient using multiplication because division and multiplication are inverse, or opposite, operations.

$\boxed{} \times 4 = \frac{1}{3}$

2. A teacher shares $\frac{1}{2}$ of a box of pencils equally among 3 children. What fraction of all the pencils in the box does each child get? $\frac{1}{2} \div 3$

$\frac{1}{2} \div 3 = \boxed{}$

Each child gets $\boxed{}$ of the pencils in the box.

Check the quotient using multiplication: $\boxed{} \times 3 = \frac{1}{2}$

Note for student: You can develop your own strategies to divide fractions by reasoning about the relationship between multiplication and division.

3. If I have $\frac{1}{4}$ of a pizza and I share it equally with a friend, what fraction of the whole pizza do we each get?

$\frac{1}{4} \div 2$

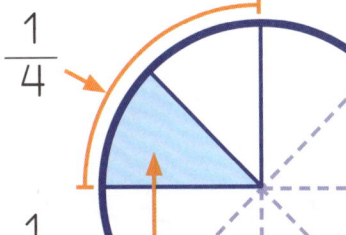

$\frac{1}{4} \div 2 = \dfrac{\boxed{}}{\boxed{}}$

We each get $\dfrac{\boxed{}}{\boxed{}}$ of the whole pizza.

Check the quotient using multiplication: $\dfrac{\boxed{}}{\boxed{}} \times 2 = \dfrac{\boxed{}}{\boxed{}}$

4. Jamal shares $\frac{1}{3}$ of a box of dog biscuits equally among his 3 dogs. What fraction of all the biscuits in the box does each dog get?

$\frac{1}{3} \div 3$

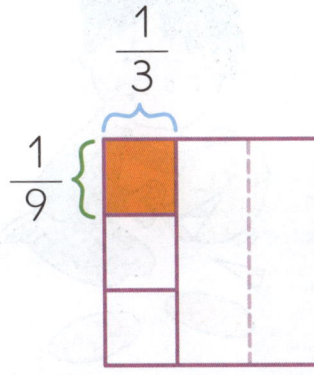

$\frac{1}{3} \div 3 = \dfrac{\boxed{}}{\boxed{}}$

Each dog gets $\dfrac{\boxed{}}{\boxed{}}$ of all the biscuits in the box.

Check the quotient using multiplication: $\dfrac{\boxed{}}{\boxed{}} \times 3 = \dfrac{\boxed{}}{\boxed{}}$

83

Divide a Whole Number by a Fraction

Read the problems and use the models to find the quotients.

1. I have 4 lengths of fabric and I cut each length into fifths. How many fifths do I have all together?

$4 \div \dfrac{1}{5}$

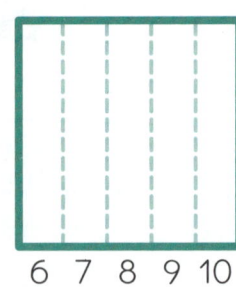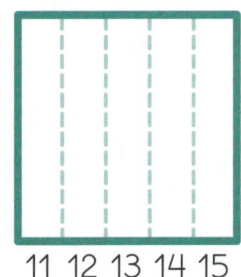

1 2 3 4 5   6 7 8 9 10   11 12 13 14 15   16 17 18 19 20

$4 \div \dfrac{1}{5} = 20$

Check the quotient using multiplication: ☐ $\times \dfrac{1}{5} = 4$

2. I have 3 circles and I cut each circle into eighths. How many eighths do I have all together?

$3 \div \dfrac{1}{8}$

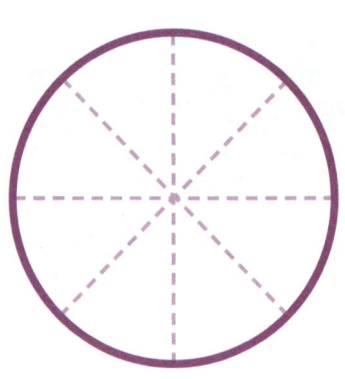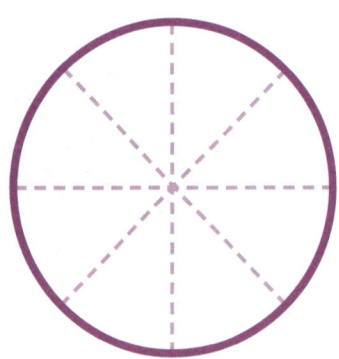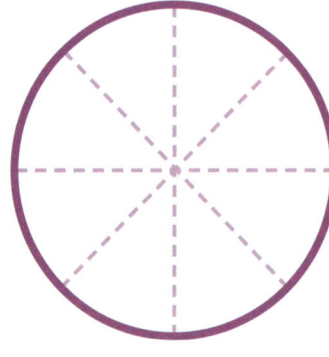

$3 \div \dfrac{1}{8} = $ ☐

Check the quotient using multiplication: ☐ $\times \dfrac{1}{8} = 3$

Note for student: This activity is an introduction to the division of fractions, which is a topic that you will develop further in sixth grade.

3. I have 3 loaves and I divide each loaf into sixths. How many sixths do I have all together?

$3 \div \frac{1}{6}$

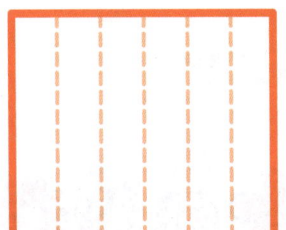 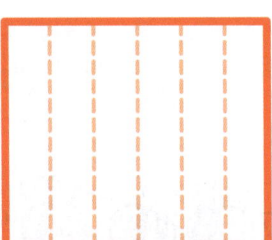 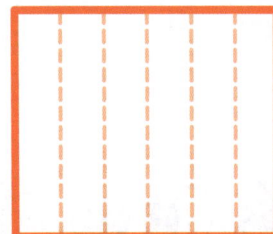

$3 \div \frac{1}{6} = \square$

Check the quotient using multiplication: $\square \times \frac{1}{6} = \square$

4. I have 4 squares and I divide each square into quarters. How many quarters do I have all together?

$4 \div \frac{1}{4}$

$4 \div \frac{1}{4} = \square$

Check the quotient using multiplication: $\square \times \frac{1}{4} = \square$

85

Understanding Ratio

A ratio is how many times greater one quantity is to another quantity. In the example below, the ratio of frogs to fish is 1 to 4.

We can write this ratio as **1 : 4**

The colon in the middle means "to."

Figure out these ratios:

1. What is the ratio of flowers to bees?

☐ flowers to ☐ bees = ☐ : ☐

2. What is the ratio of chocolate cookies to cupcakes?

☐ chocolate cookies to ☐ cupcakes = ☐ : ☐

3. What is the ratio of pentagons to triangles?

☐ pentagons to ☐ triangles = ☐ : ☐

4. What is the ratio of blue pens to red pens?

☐ blue pens to ☐ red pens = ☐ : ☐

Note for student: This activity introduces the concept of ratio, and the language we use to describe ratios.

Ratio Tables

For every 1 milkshake bought at Dino's Diner, the customer is given 2 free cookies.

The ratio is **1 : 2**

How many free cookies are given with 2 milkshakes?

☐ cookies

You can draw a ratio table to help you work out the answer to this type of problem.

Milkshakes	1	2	3	4	7	10	15	22
Cookies	2							

×2
×3
×4
×7

Complete the table above, then use it to answer the following questions.

1. How many milkshakes would you have to buy to get 20 cookies?

☐ milkshakes

2. How many cookies would you get for 7 milkshakes?

☐ cookies

3. If Tyler bought 15 milkshakes in a month, how many cookies did he get?

☐ cookies

4. If Tara had 44 cookies, how many milkshakes did she buy?

☐ milkshakes

Note for student: A ratio table is a useful tool that you can use to calculate ratios.

Ratio Problems

Figure out the answers to these problems. Use the ratio tables to help you find the answers.

1. For every 5 oranges that Mia sells at her market stall, she sells 1 apple. What is the ratio of oranges to apples sold?

If she sells 50 oranges, how many apples are sold?

Oranges	5	50
Apples	1	

[ ] oranges sold : [ ] apple sold

50 oranges sold : [ ] apples sold

2. To make 1 liter of fresh orange juice, Rico uses 8 oranges. How many oranges will he use to make 4 liters?

Oranges	8	
Liters of juice	1	4

[ ] oranges : [ ] liter

[ ] oranges : 4 liters

3. Rosa's pizza recipe has a ratio of 5 cups of flour to 2 cups of water. How many cups of water will she need to add to 15 cups of flour?

Cups of flour	5	15
Cups of water	2	

[ ] cups of flour : [ ] cups of water

15 cups of flour : [ ] cups of water

Note for student: This activity helps you to see how you can use ratio to solve everyday problems.

Equivalent Ratios

When we multiply or divide the ratio by the same number we get equivalent ratios.
We can size up a ratio using multiplication, or size down a ratio using division. For example, to size down 10:50 we can divide by 10 because 10 is the greatest common factor.

10 : 50 = 1 : 5   Divide by 10

The word "equivalent" means "the same." Equivalent ratios are ratios with the same value.

Example
If I mix 3 cans of blue paint with 4 cans of yellow paint, this gives me a ratio of 3:4

  :

Which ratio of blue paint to yellow paint has the same value as the ratio 3:4? Circle the correct ratio.

4 : 3   2 : 3   6 : 12   12 : 14   9 : 12

You can use a ratio table to find equivalent ratios. Complete the ratio table.

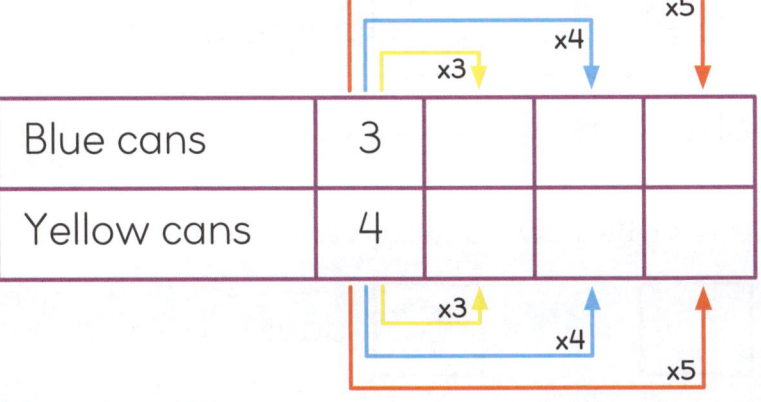

Draw circles around 4 equivalent ratios below.

8 : 2   4 : 1   60 : 20
      16 : 4   80 : 20
            20 : 10
10 : 4   50 : 10

Note for student: A ratio table will help you to organize your thinking around ratios, and help you to see patterns in number sequences.

Understanding Rate

A rate is a ratio that usually involves a measurement of time.

Example
If it takes Luis 6 hours to mow 4 lawns, the rate is 6 hours ÷ 4 lawns. This is a rate of **1.5** (or $1\frac{1}{2}$) lawns mowed per hour.

The word "**per**" means each or every. "**Per hour**" means each or every hour.

Calculate the following rates.

1. Izzy is writing a book about space. She writes 70 pages in 5 days. Calculate the rate per day.

70 ÷ ☐ = ☐ pages per day

She writes at a rate of ☐ pages per day

At this rate, how many days will it take her to write 56 pages?

☐ ÷ 14 = ☐ days

If Izzy finishes her book when she reaches 168 pages, how many days in total does it take her to write her book?

168 ÷ ☐ = ☐ days

Note for student: Try to think up more math problems such as these to give further practice.

2. Jamal is training for a race. He runs 15 miles in 6 hours, at what rate does Jamal run?

15 ÷ ☐ = ☐ miles per hour

He runs at a rate of ☐ miles per hour

On the next day of training, Jamal runs 15 miles at a rate of 3 miles per hour, what is his race time in hours?

15 ÷ ☐ = ☐ hours

Jamal ran the race in ☐ hours

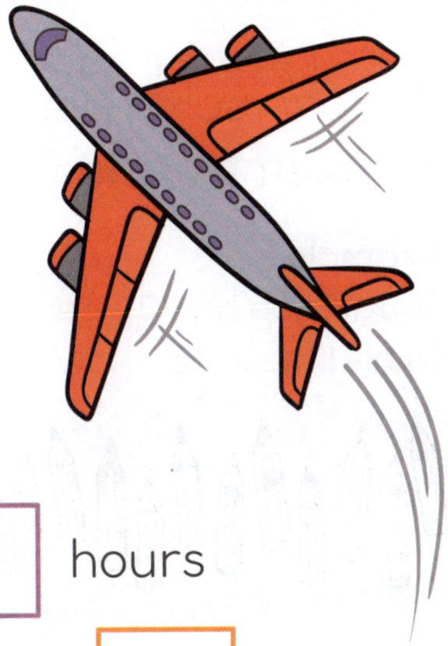

---

3. If a passenger plane travels at 500 miles per hour, how long would it take to reach a destination 800 miles away?

800 mi ÷ ☐ mi/h = time

We can simplify the numbers to make it easier. → 8 ÷ 5 = ☐ hours

Now convert the decimal to find minutes. → 0.6 of 60 minutes = ☐ minutes

Or, we could write this problem as a fraction. → $\frac{8}{\square} = 1\frac{\square}{5}$ hours

Now convert the fraction part to find minutes. → $\frac{3}{5}$ of 60 minutes = ☐ minutes

☐ hour ☐ minutes

Percentages

Finding a percentage of a quantity is like finding a fraction of an amount. A percentage is a type of fraction that always has 100 as the denominator.

$$50\% = \frac{50}{100} \xrightarrow{\text{Simplify}} \frac{\div 50}{\div 50} = \frac{1}{2}$$

50% of a quantity means $\frac{1}{2}$

50% of my pizza is half of my pizza.

We can solve percentage problems using fractions.

Remember "**per**" means each or every, and "**cent**" means 100. So "**percent**" means per 100.

Example
If Jackson had 24 pencils and gave 50% of these to his little sister, how many pencils did he give her?

50% of 24 = ☐ pencils

As a fraction we write $\frac{\Box}{100} \times 24$ Simplify $\frac{1}{2} \times \frac{\Box}{1} = \frac{24}{2} = \Box$

50% of 24 means 50% × 24

24 written as a fraction is: $\frac{24}{1}$

Answer: Jackson gave his sister ☐ pencils.

Note for student: There are often different ways of solving the same problem, and you can choose the method that is easiest for you.

92

Solve the following percentage problems using fractions.

1. A baseball team played 15 games, and won 60% of them. How many games did they win?

$$\frac{\boxed{60}}{100} \times \frac{15}{1} \xrightarrow{\text{Simplify}} \frac{\boxed{3}}{5} \times \frac{15}{1} = \frac{45}{5} = \boxed{9}$$

They won $\boxed{9}$ games.

2. A coat priced at $48 was reduced by 25% in the sale. How much was the discount in dollars?

$$\frac{\boxed{25}}{100} \times \frac{48}{1} \xrightarrow{\text{Simplify}} \frac{1}{\boxed{4}} \times \frac{48}{1} = \frac{\boxed{48}}{4} = \boxed{12}$$

The discount was $ $\boxed{12}$

How much did the coat cost after the discount?

After discount, the coat cost $ $\boxed{36}$

3. A baker sold 70 cookies. 30% of the cookies sold were chocolate. How many chocolate cookies did he sell?

$$\frac{\boxed{30}}{100} \times \frac{70}{1} \xrightarrow{\text{Simplify}} \frac{\boxed{3}}{10} \times \frac{70}{1} = \frac{\boxed{210}}{10} = \boxed{21}$$

He sold $\boxed{21}$ chocolate cookies.

Measurement, Data, and Geometry

Student Notes

The activities in this section will help you learn how to:

- Measure length, weight, and capacity using standard US units and metric units of measurement.

- Sort mathematical shapes, and calculate the volume of regular and irregular 3D shapes.

- Use negative numbers, and make calculations of mean, median, and range in statistics.

You may choose to work on the activities independently, or you may want help from a parent or other adult at the start of an activity.

Contents

Length Conversions	96	Coordinates and Compass Points	110
Metric Length Conversions	97	Negative Numbers	112
Weight Conversions	98	Minus Temperatures	114
Metric Weight Conversions	99	Negative Number Problems	115
Capacity Conversions	100	Negative Coordinates	116
Metric Capacity Conversions	101	Finding the Mean	118
Graphing Data on Line Plots	102	Finding the Median	120
Quadrilaterals Family Tree	104	Mean, Median, and Range	121
Sorting Shapes	105	More Mean Data Problems	122
Volume—Cubic Units	106	Answers	127
Volume of an Irregular Shape	108		

Length Conversions

Length is a measurement of something from end to end. We can measure length in customary units. Remember these conversions:

12 inches (in.) = 1 foot (ft.)   3 feet = 1 yard (yd.)
36 inches = 1 yard (yd.)   1,760 yards = 1 mile (mi.)

When we convert measurements from one unit of measure to another we have to decide whether we need to multiply or divide.

- When we go from a *larger* unit (e.g., feet) to a smaller unit (e.g., inches) we *multiply*.
- When we go from a *smaller* unit (e.g., inches) to a larger unit (e.g., feet) we *divide*.

1. How do we convert 6 feet to inches? We know that feet are *larger* than inches so we *multiply*.

6 x 12 = ☐ in.

Multiply by 12 to convert to inches.

2. How do we convert 48 inches to feet? We know that inches are *smaller* than feet so we *divide*.

48 ÷ 12 = ☐ ft.

Divide by 12 to convert to feet.

Convert these measurements.

3. 60 in. = ☐ ft. → because 60 ÷ 12 = ☐

4. 10 ft. = ☐ in. → because 10 x 12 = ☐

5. 15 yd. = ☐ ft. → because 15 x ☐ = ☐

6. 99 ft. = ☐ yd. → because 99 ÷ ☐ = ☐

Note for student: When you multiply in a conversion you get a greater number of units, but when you divide the result is fewer units.

Metric Length Conversions

We can measure length in metric units. Remember these conversions:

 "centi" means $\frac{1}{100}$ and "milli" means $\frac{1}{1,000}$

10 millimeters (mm) = 1 centimeter (cm)
100 centimeters = 1 meter (m)
1,000 meters = 1 kilometer (km)

How do we convert 1.5 cm to mm? We know that centimeters are *larger* than millimeters so we *multiply*.

1.5 cm = 15 mm

Multiply by 10 to convert to millimeters. The decimal point moves 1 place to the right.

How we convert 5 cm to m? We know that centimeters are *smaller* than meters so we *divide*.

5. cm = 0.05 m

Divide by 100 to convert to meters. The decimal point moves 2 places to the left.

Convert these measurements:

Sometimes we need to add one or more zeros as placeholders when we move a decimal point. If there is no decimal point shown, it is at the end of the number.

1. 6 m = ☐ cm
2. 16.5 cm = ☐ mm
3. 0.6 km = ☐ m
4. 6,000 m = ☐ km

Note for student: Remember, you need to convert different units of measurement to the same unit measurements.

Weight Conversions

Weight (or mass) is a measurement of how heavy something is. We can measure weight in customary units. Remember these conversions:

16 ounces (oz.) = 1 pound (lb.)   2,000 pounds (lb.) = 1 ton (tn.)

1. How do we convert 20 oz. to lb.? We know that ounces are *smaller* than pounds so we *divide*.

    20 ÷ 16 = ☐ lb. ☐ oz.

    Divide by 16 to convert to pounds.

2. How do we convert 12 lb. to oz.? We know that pounds are *larger* than ounces so we *multiply*.

    12 x 16 = ☐ oz.

    Multiply by 16 to convert to ounces.

Convert these measurements.

3. 50 lb. = ☐ oz. → because 50 x 16 = ☐

4. 96 oz. = ☐ lb. → because 96 ÷ 16 = ☐

5. 6 tn. = ☐ lb. → because 6 x ☐ = ☐

6. 8,000 lb. = ☐ tn. → because 8,000 ÷ ☐ = ☐

7. 224 oz. = ☐ lb. → because 224 ÷ ☐ = ☐

8. 25 tn. = ☐ lb. → because 25 x ☐ = ☐

Note for student: Always check that your answers are reasonable by using a rough estimate.

Metric Weight Conversions

We can measure weight in metric units. Remember this conversion:

1,000 grams (g) = 1 kilogram (kg)

How do we convert 7.5 kg to g?

7.5 = 7,500 g

We multiply by 1,000 to convert to grams so we move the decimal point 3 places to the right, and add 2 zeros as placeholders. We don't need to put the decimal point at the end of the number.

This book weighs 800 g = 0.8 kg

How we convert 7,500 g to kg?

7,500 g = 7.5 kg

We divide by 1,000 to convert to kilograms so the decimal point moves 3 places to the left.

1. How do we convert 5,000 g to kg? We know that grams are *smaller* than kilograms so we *divide*.

5,000 ÷ 1,000 = ☐ kg

Divide by 1,000 to convert to kilograms.

2. How do we convert 7 kg to g? We know that kilograms are *larger* than grams so we *multiply*.

7 × 1,000 = ☐ g

Multiply by 1,000 to convert to grams.

Convert these measurements.

3. 6 kg = ☐ g

4. 4,000 g = ☐ kg

5. 5.5 kg = ☐ g

6. 3,500 g = ☐ kg

Note for student: When you multiply the decimal point moves to the right, and when you divide the decimal point moves to the left.

Capacity Conversions

Capacity is a measurement of how much something holds. We can measure capacity in customary units. Remember these conversions:

> 8 fluid ounces (fl. oz.) = 1 cup (c.)   2 cups = 1 pint (pt.)
> 2 pints = 4 cups, or 1 quart (qt.)   4 quarts = 1 gallon (gal.)

Try to visualize how many of these customary units are equal to 1 gallon.

G = QQQQ = PPPPPPPP = CCCC CCCC CCCC CCCC = (128 o's)

1 gallon = 4 quarts = 8 pints = 16 cups = 128 fluid ounces

Use the model above to convert these measurements.

1. 3 gal. = ☐ pt.

   8 pt. = 1 gal. so we multiply 3 × 8

2. 3 qt. = ☐ c.

3. 10 gal. = ☐ qt.

4. $\frac{1}{2}$ gal. = ☐ pt.

5. 32 c. = ☐ gal.

6. 32 pt. = ☐ gal.

> One fluid ounce is like 6 teaspoons.

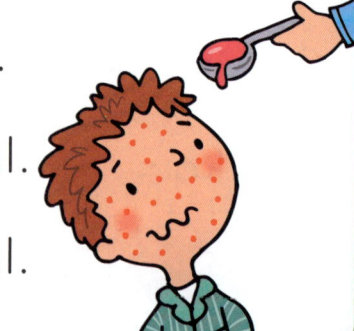

Note for student: The capacity table above is designed to help you remember the facts.

Metric Capacity Conversions

We can measure capacity in metric units. Remember these conversions:

500 milliliters (mL) = 0.5 liter (L)
1,000 milliliters (mL) = 1 liter (L)

Study this conversion table:

Quantity in mL	Quantity in L	As a Fraction
250 mL	0.25 L	$\frac{1}{4}$ L
500 mL	0.50 L	$\frac{1}{2}$ L
750 mL	0.75 L	$\frac{3}{4}$ L
1,000 mL	1 L	$\frac{1}{1}$ L

Remember 0.50 and 0.5 have the same value. Sometimes we write 0.50 with 0 as a placeholder after the 5 for column calculations and tables.

Try to work out these conversions for yourself:

Quantity in mL	Quantity in L	As a Fraction
100 mL	0.10 L	
200 mL		$\frac{2}{10}$ L or $\frac{1}{5}$ L
300 mL		$\frac{3}{10}$ L
400 mL	0.40 L	
800 mL		$\frac{8}{10}$ L or $\frac{4}{5}$ L
1,100 mL		$1\frac{1}{10}$ L

Note for student: Think about these useful comparisons: a drip from a tap is about a milliliter, and two small bottles of water are approximately a liter.

Graphing Data on Line Plots

Mia collected data to find out how much rain fell over a period of 14 days. Graph Mia's data in a line plot. Write an X on the line plot to represent the amount of rain on the inches scale.

Day 1	Day 2	Day 3	Day 4	Day 5	Day 6	Day 7
1	1	$1\frac{1}{2}$	$\frac{1}{2}$	$1\frac{3}{4}$	$1\frac{1}{4}$	0

Day 8	Day 9	Day 10	Day 11	Day 12	Day 13	Day 14
0	$1\frac{3}{4}$	$\frac{1}{2}$	$2\frac{1}{4}$	$1\frac{1}{2}$	4	4

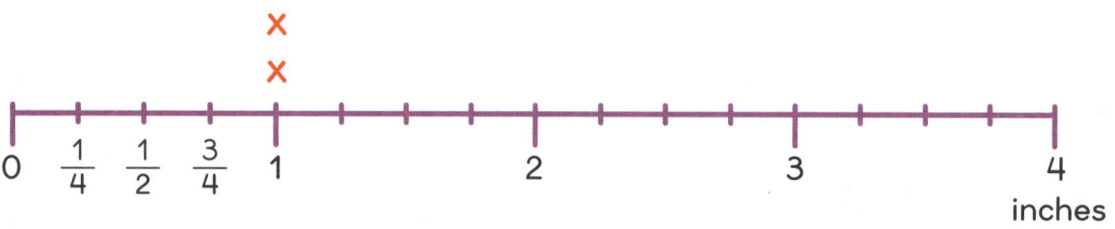

Answer these questions by studying the data in the your completed line plot.

1. What was the most rain to fall in one day? .... in.
2. How many days had no rainfall? .... days
3. How many days had 2 or more inches of rain? .... days
4. How much rain fell in total over the 14 days? .... in.
Add together all the amounts. Group the numbers to make addition easier:

← Super-challenging question!

$$1 + 1 + 1\frac{1}{2} + \frac{1}{2} + 1\frac{3}{4} + 1\frac{1}{4} + 1\frac{3}{4} + \frac{1}{2} + 2\frac{1}{4} + 1\frac{1}{2} + 4 + 4 =$$

$$4 \quad + \quad 3 \quad + \quad 2\frac{1}{4} \quad + \quad 3\frac{3}{4} \quad + \quad 8 \quad =$$

Now regroup again:

$$4 + 3 + 2\frac{1}{4} + 3\frac{3}{4} + 8 =$$

$$7 \quad + \quad 6 \quad + \quad 8 \quad = \boxed{}$$

Note for student: A line plot is a useful graph that shows scientific and mathematical data.

This table lists the lengths of 11 tadpoles in a garden pond. Graph the data in a line plot. Write an X on the line plot to represent the length of each tadpole on the inches scale.

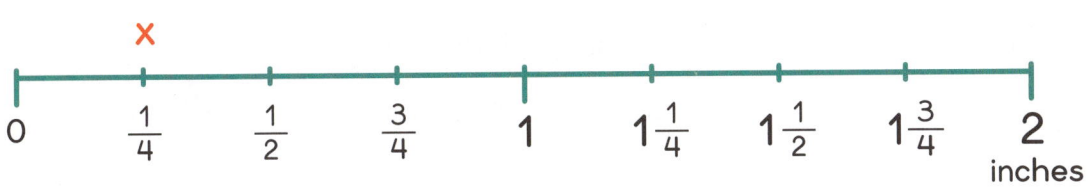

Answer these questions by studying the data in the your completed line plot.

1. What length is the longest tadpole? .... in.

2. What is the length of the shortest tadpole? .... in.

3. What is the difference in length between the longest tadpole and the shortest tadpole? .... in.

4. If all the tadpoles swam in a long line, head to tail, how long would the line of tadpoles be? .... in.

Super-challenging calculation!

Add together all the amounts. Group the numbers to make addition easier:

$(\frac{1}{4} + \frac{1}{2}) + (\frac{3}{4} \times 3) + (1 \times 4) + (1\frac{1}{2} \times 2) =$

$\frac{3}{4} + 2\frac{1}{4} + 4 + 3 = \boxed{}$

5. If a fish ate half of this line of tadpoles, what length would be left? .... in.

Quadrilaterals Family Tree

Study the quadrilaterals family tree then answer the questions below.

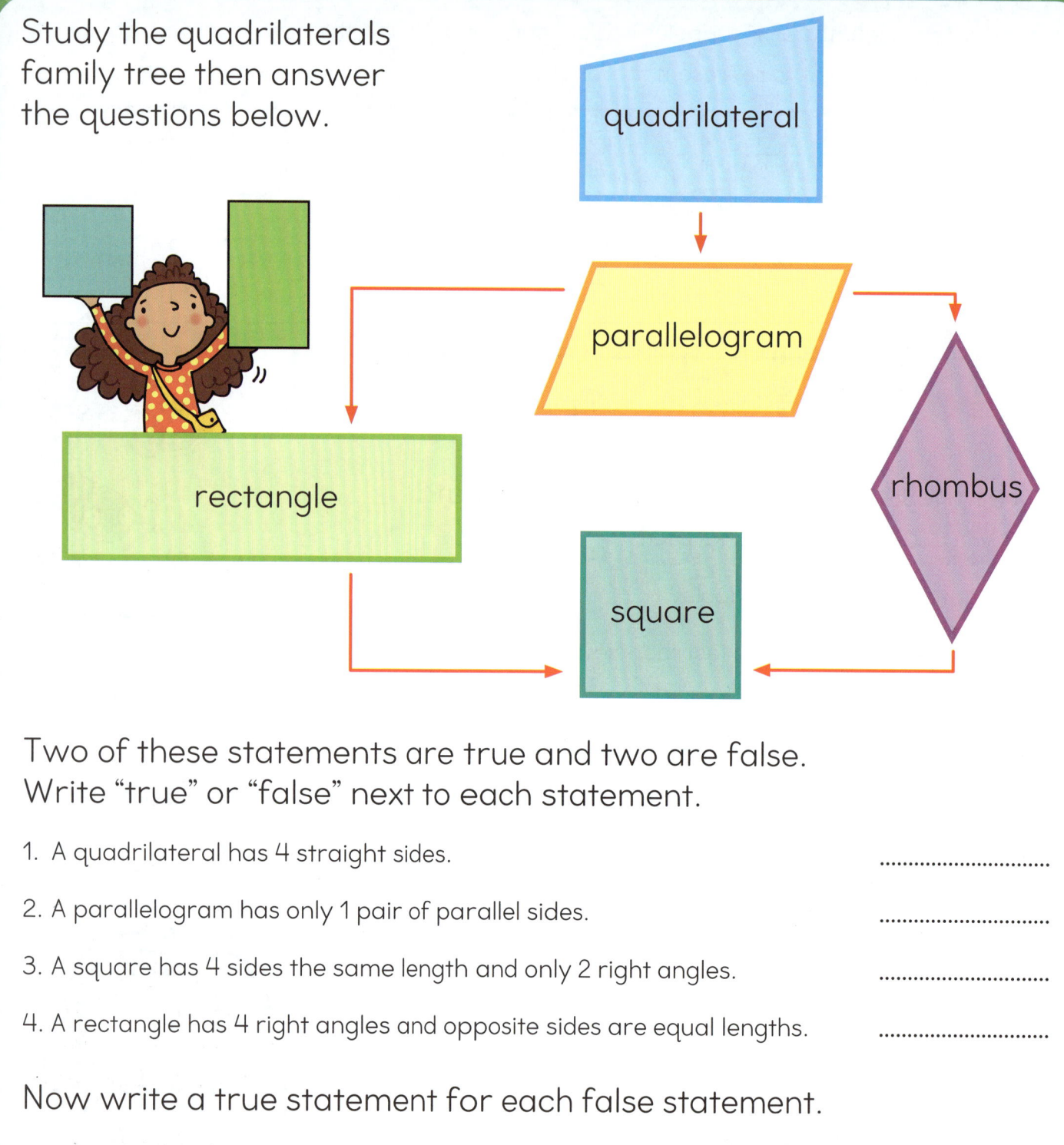

Two of these statements are true and two are false. Write "true" or "false" next to each statement.

1. A quadrilateral has 4 straight sides. ....
2. A parallelogram has only 1 pair of parallel sides. ....
3. A square has 4 sides the same length and only 2 right angles. ....
4. A rectangle has 4 right angles and opposite sides are equal lengths. ....

Now write a true statement for each false statement.

1. ....
2. ....

Note for student: This activity is a refresh of quadrilaterals and their properties.

Sorting Shapes

The square belongs to both the rhombus group and the rectangle group, just like Jackson who belongs to both the soccer team and the baseball team.

rhombuses: 4 sides the same length and equal opposite angles

squares: 4 sides the same length and 4 right angles

rectangles: 4 right angles and opposite sides are equal lengths

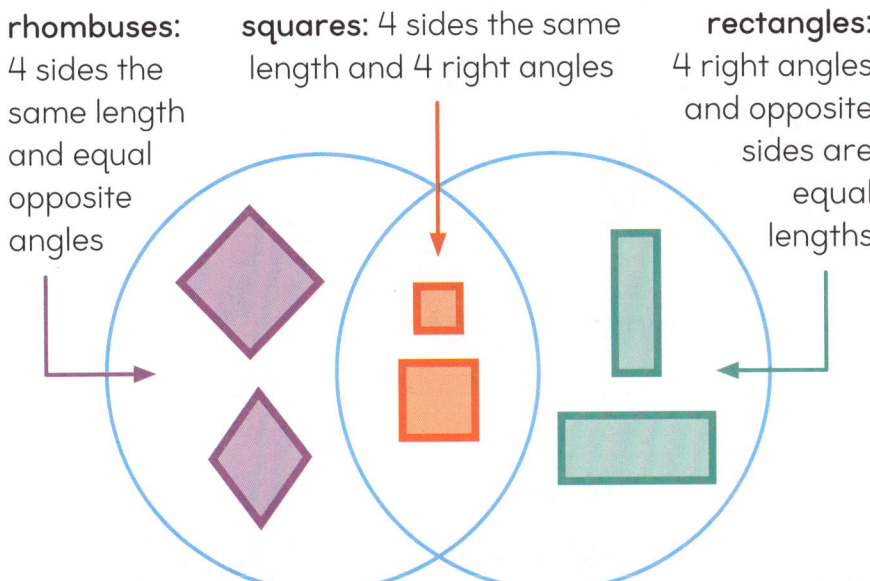

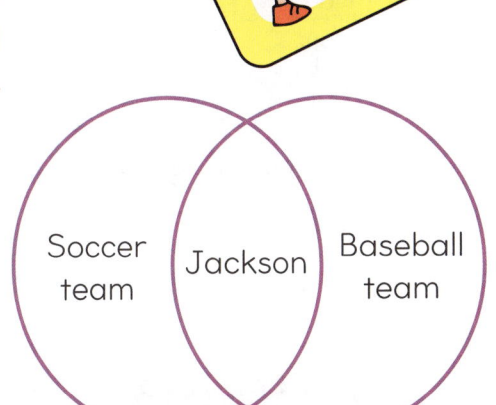

Copy the names of the shapes into the correct groups in the table below. Some shapes may belong to more than one group. One shape belongs to all three groups!

parallelogram   square   regular hexagon   rhombus
equilateral triangle   rectangle

Shapes with 2 pairs of parallel sides	Shapes with all sides the same length	Shapes with 4 right angles

Note for student: Shapes can belong to more than one group depending on how the groups are classified or described.

105

Volume—Cubic Units

Volume is how much space a three-dimensional (3D) object takes up.

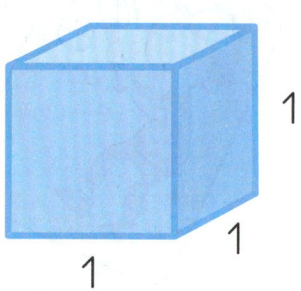

This cube is a 3D object. Each of its sides measures 1 unit so we call it a "unit cube." It has a volume of one cubic unit. We can use it to measure volume.

Look at the 3D shape, A, below. It is made up of layers of cubes, and there are no gaps or overlaps. Count the cubes in the layers to find the volume of the shape.

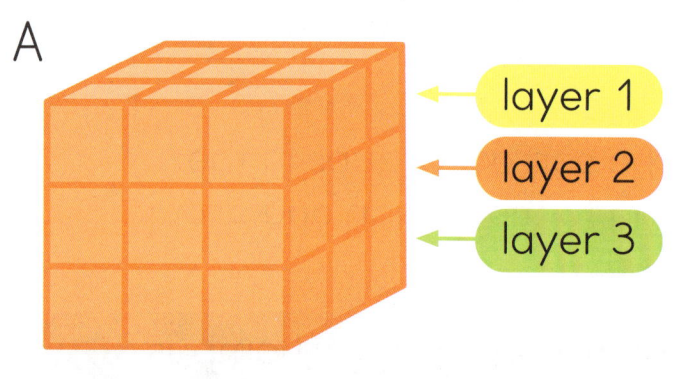

Volume = layer 1 + layer 2 + layer 3

Volume =

☐ + ☐ + ☐

= ☐ cubic units

Try this prism shape, B. Count how many cubes in the top layer then multiply by the total number of layers.

Volume =

☐ × ☐ = ☐ cubic units

Note for student: Sometimes you will see cubic units (or cu) written as 3 in superscript. For instance, ft.³, m³, etc.

Sometimes it's not easy to count layers in a 3D shape so we use a formula instead. To find the volume of the containers pictured below we can use this formula:

Volume (V): Multiply the length (l) by the width (w) by the height (h). We write this as **V = l x w x h**

Try this formula to figure out the volumes of these containers.

1. A cereal box is 20 inches long, by 10 inches wide, by 20 inches high. What is its volume?

    Volume =
    ☐ x ☐ x ☐ = ☐ cubic inches

    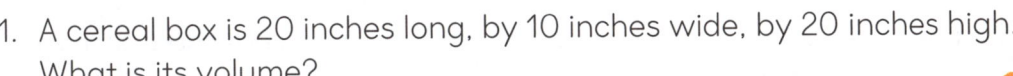

2. A candy box is 5 centimeters long, by 5 centimeters wide, by 15 centimeters high. What is its volume?

    Volume =
    ☐ x ☐ x ☐ = ☐ cubic centimeters

    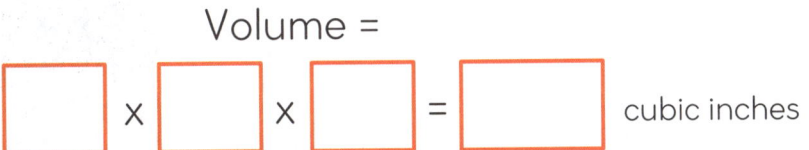

3. A shipping container is 20 feet long, by 8 feet wide, by 8 feet high. What is the volume of the container?

    Volume =
    ☐ x ☐ x ☐ = ☐ cubic feet

107

Volume of an Irregular Shape

Sometimes we need to find the volume of an irregular or composite shape.

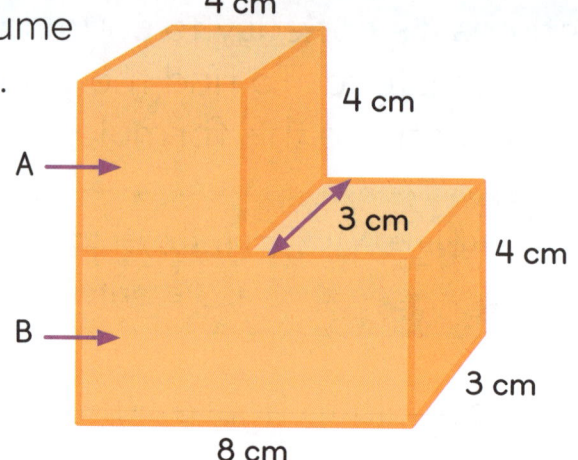

1. Two rectangular prisms have been put together to create the composite shape to the right. What is the total volume of this shape?

Use the formula $V = l \times w \times h$ to figure out the volume of each prism. Treat them as two separate shapes, A and B, then add the volumes together.

Volume of A = ☐ × ☐ × ☐ = ☐ cm³

Volume of B = ☐ × ☐ × ☐ = ☐ cm³

Total volume = Volume of A + B = ☐ cm³

2. Find the volume of this composite shape.

Volume of A = ☐ × ☐ × ☐ = ☐ m³

Volume of B = ☐ × ☐ × ☐ = ☐ m³

Total volume = Volume of A + B = ☐ m³

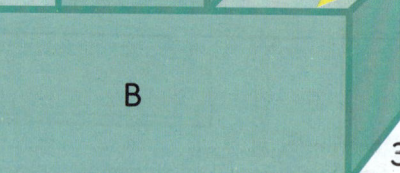

Remember superscript ³ is an abbreviation for "cubic units."

Note for student: This activity shows you how you can use math to solve everyday problems relating to volume.

Now try these word problems.

1. A desk caddy has a section for crayons measuring 10 inches long, 3 inches wide, and 4 inches high. It also has a section for pencils measuring 3 inches long, 3 inches wide, and 8 inches high. What is the total volume of the desk caddy?

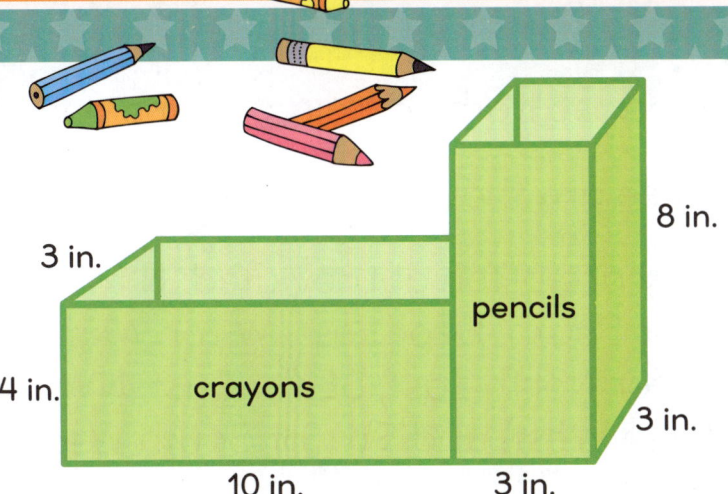

Volume of crayons = ☐ × ☐ × ☐ = ☐ in.³

Volume of pencils = ☐ × ☐ × ☐ = ☐ in.³

Total volume = ☐ + ☐ = ☐ in.³

2. A closet measures 4 feet long, 2 feet wide, and 7 feet high. Next to it there is a cupboard which measures 3 feet long, 2 feet wide, and 5 feet high. What is the total volume of the storage?

Volume of closet = ☐ × ☐ × ☐ = ☐ ft.³

Volume of cupboard = ☐ × ☐ × ☐ = ☐ ft.³

Total volume = ☐ + ☐ = ☐ ft.³

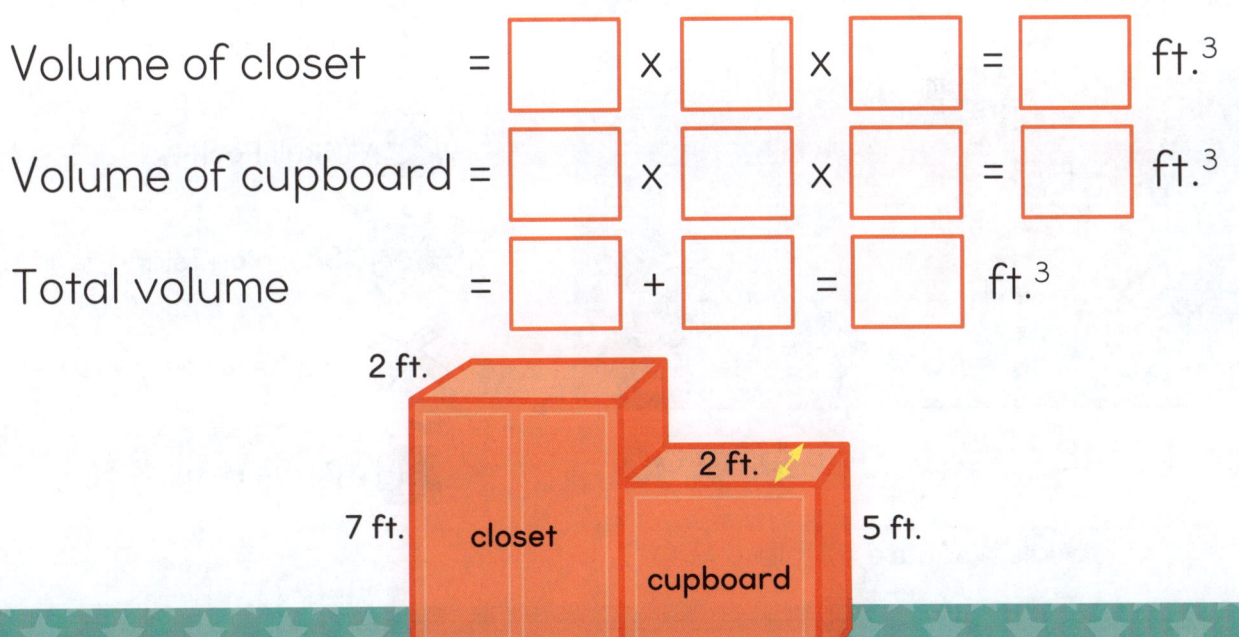

Coordinates and Compass Points

Maps use both coordinates and compass points.

These are the points of the compass.

They are often abbreviated: **N** for North, **S** for South, **E** for East, **W** for West, **NE** for North East, **SE** for East, **NW** for North West, and **SW** for South West.

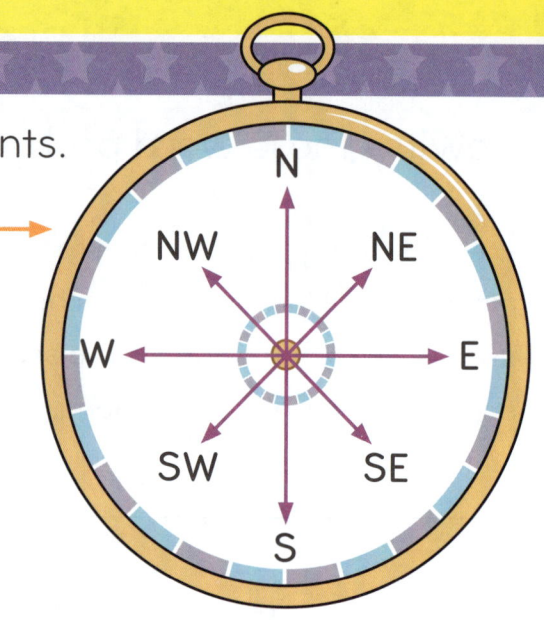

We can use compass points to say where something is located, or to say which way something is going. For example, the crocodile swamp is SW of the pirate treasure.

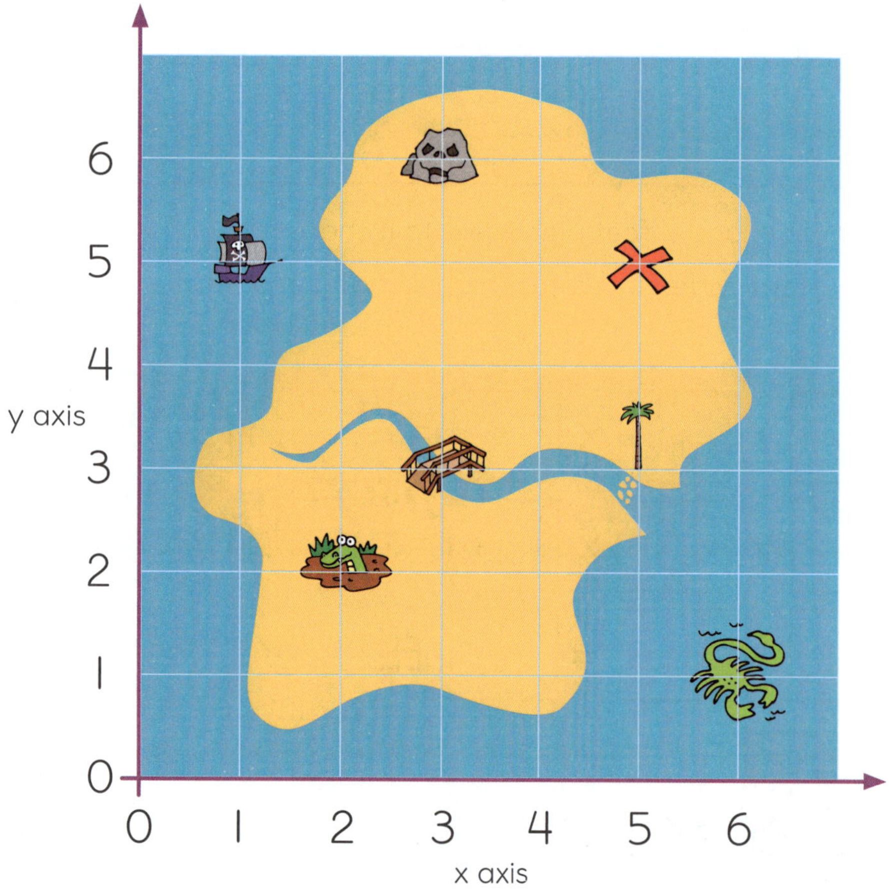

Key
- Crocodile swamp
- Footbridge
- Tall palm tree
- Skull Rock
- Scorpion Island
- Dig here for treasure!
- Pirate ship

Scale: 1 square = 1 mile

Note for student: Learning how to read coordinates and compass points is a useful life skill.

Write the coordinates for the following locations.

Pirate ship = (......... , ...)   Crocodile swamp = (......... , ...)

Scorpion Island = (......... , ...)

Draw your route on the map and write the missing coordinates as you follow these directions.

Start at (2 , 1), walk one square North East to reach (......... , ...). Look out for crocodiles! Walk one square North to the footbridge at (......... , ...), then continue North three squares to reach Skull Rock at (......... , ...). Walk one square East to (......... , ...), then walk one square South East to dig for the treasure at (......... , ...)! Now make your way back. Walk two squares South to the tall palm tree at (......... , ...). The river is shallow enough to cross. Continue one square South West to (......... , ...) then walk one square South to (......... , ...). Walk two squares West to reach (......... , ...), back where you started from.

Write the number of miles and the compass direction.

1. Where is the treasure in relation to the tall palm tree?   [2] miles   North

2. Where is the footbridge in relation to Skull Rock?   [ ] miles   ....

3. Where is the tall palm tree in relation to the footbridge?   [ ] miles   ....

4. Where is the pirate ship in relation to the treasure?   [ ] miles   ....

111

Negative Numbers

Negative numbers are numbers less than zero. It's hard to imagine a number less than zero, but there are many examples in the real world.

Temperatures can fall below zero.
Winter temperatures in Alaska normally range from 0°F to -30°F (-18°C to -35°C.)

 °F = degrees Fahrenheit
°C = degrees Celsius

We can write negative numbers on a number line. Numbers to the right of zero are positive and numbers to the left of zero are negative.

Money in a bank account can go below zero. If you have -5 dollars in your bank account you owe the bank 5 dollars!

Opposite numbers are at the same distance from zero on the number line, but go in opposite directions. The opposite of -1 is 1. The opposite of -2 is 2, and so on.

1. Complete these number lines.

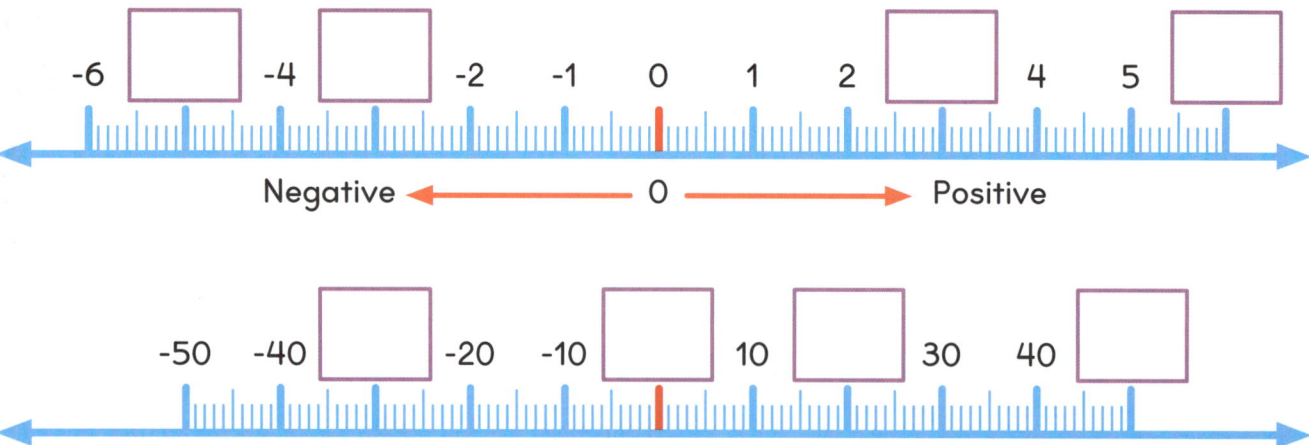

Note for student: This activity helps you to see how negative numbers are used in everyday life.

2. Draw an arrow to mark the approximate position of these numbers on the number line below. The first one has been done for you.

-2.2   3.5   -5.4   -1.9   -6.6   -4.1

3. Which is warmer:
   -3°F or -7°F?

We can write this as:
   -3°F > -7°F

Remember:
> means greater than
< means less than

Which is warmer? Write the correct signs to make the statements correct.

a. 24°F ☐ -24°F   b. -80°F ☐ -88°F   c. -56°F ☐ -50°F

4. Who has the most money: Nisha who has $50 or Tasha who has $-55?

.... has the most money.

We can write: $50 > $-55

5. Write the correct signs to make the statements correct.

a. $-5 ☐ $-8   b. $-4 ☐ $4   c. $-10 ☐ $1

d. $15 ☐ $-20   e. $-7 ☐ $70   f. $50 ☐ $-25

Minus Temperatures

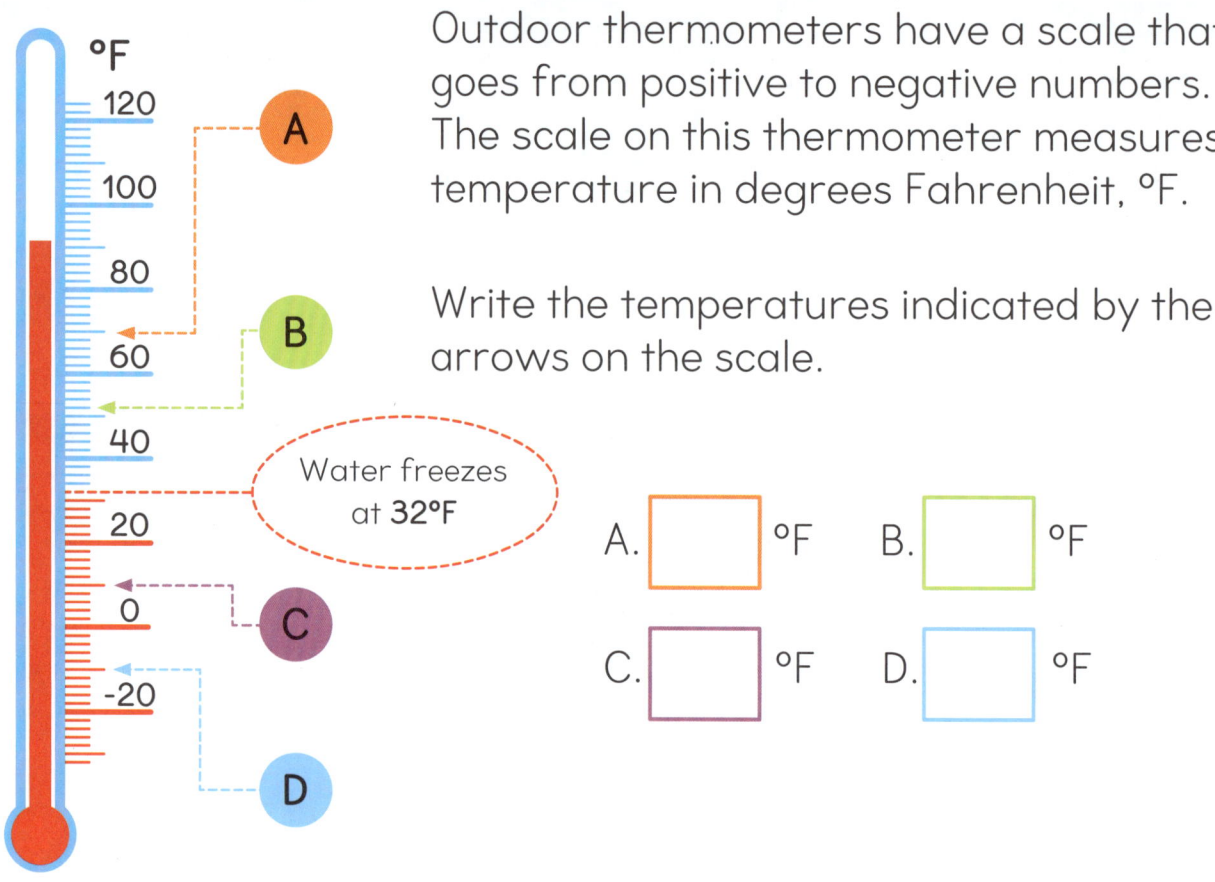

Outdoor thermometers have a scale that goes from positive to negative numbers. The scale on this thermometer measures temperature in degrees Fahrenheit, °F.

Write the temperatures indicated by the arrows on the scale.

Water freezes at **32°F**

A. ☐ °F   B. ☐ °F

C. ☐ °F   D. ☐ °F

The table below shows daytime temperatures for one day in mid-December in different cities around the world.

City	Temperature
Athens	64°F
Berlin	34°F
Copenhagen	35°F
London	42°F
Ottawa	25°F
Stockholm	31°F
Singapore	78°F
Tokyo	52°F

The coldest city is ....

The warmest city is ....

The difference in temperature between the coldest and the warmest city is

☐ °F.

Note for student: You could make comparisons with daily temperatures in your neighborhood today.

Negative Number Problems

Figure out the answers to these negative number problems. Use a separate piece of paper for your work.

1. The daytime temperature is -4°C. If the temperature falls by 8 degrees at nighttime, what will the temperature be?

The nighttime temperature will be ☐ °C

2. The temperature is -28°C. If the temperature rises by 9 degrees, what will the temperature be?

The temperature will be ☐ °C

3. Travis has 17 dollars in his bank account, but he spends 25 dollars on a shirt. How much is in his bank account now?

He will have $ ☐ in his bank account.

4. Kirsty has -15 dollars in her bank account. She puts 18 dollars into her account, but then she spends 9 dollars on a gift for her mom. How much is in her bank account now?

She will have $ ☐ in her bank account.

Note for student: You must remember that a minus quantity has a meaning or value.

115

Negative Coordinates

We often see negative numbers on coordinate grids.

1. Plot these points on the coordinate grid below. Read across the x axis first, then up or down the y axis.

(2, 3) (-4, 1) (-5, -4) (3, -3)

The **x** coordinate always comes first, just as in the alphabet **x** comes before **y**.

Plot the coordinates where the grid lines cross, not in the middle of the space between them.

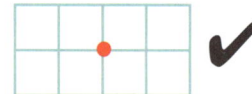

Learn the names of the quadrants:

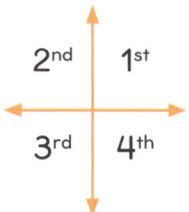

Write the name of the quadrant in which you found each of the coordinates.

(2, 3)   .... quadrant   (-4, 1)   .... quadrant

(-5, -4)   .... quadrant   (3, -3)   .... quadrant

Note for student: "Coordinates" are also referred to as "ordered pairs," and a "grid" as a "coordinate plane."

2. Plot these points on the coordinate grid, joining up the points with a line as you go along.

(-2, 3) (-4, 1) (-4, -1) (-2, -3)

(2, -3) (4, -1) (4, 1) (2, 3)

What shape have you made?

....

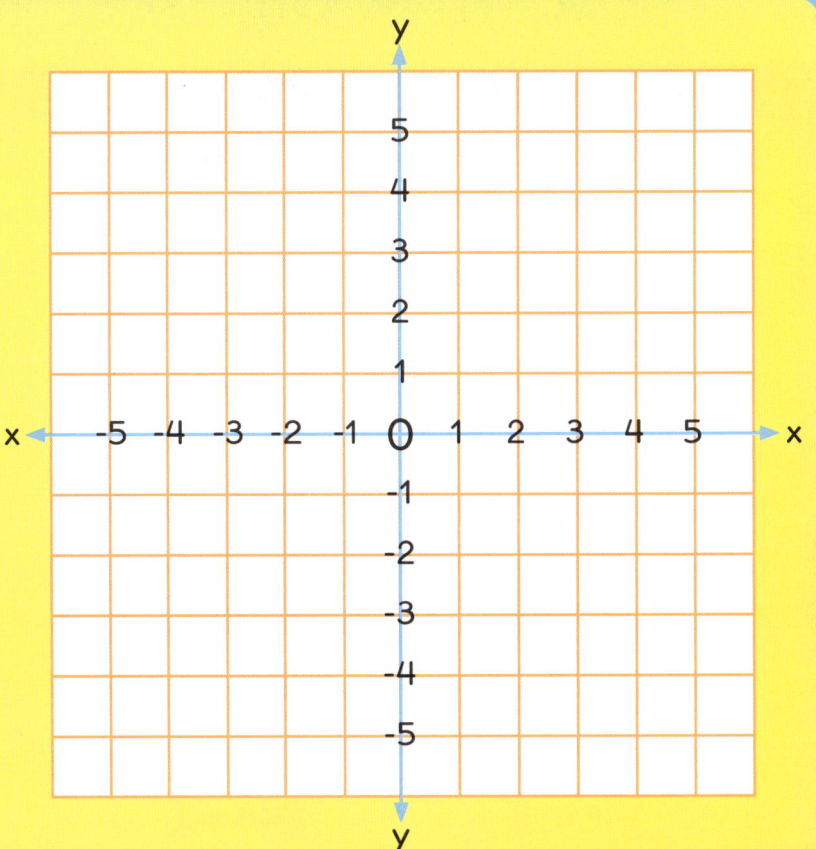

3. Use a ruler to draw a regular shape of your own on this grid. Write the coordinates for the shape you have made. Don't forget to use commas and brackets to separate the terms.

....

....

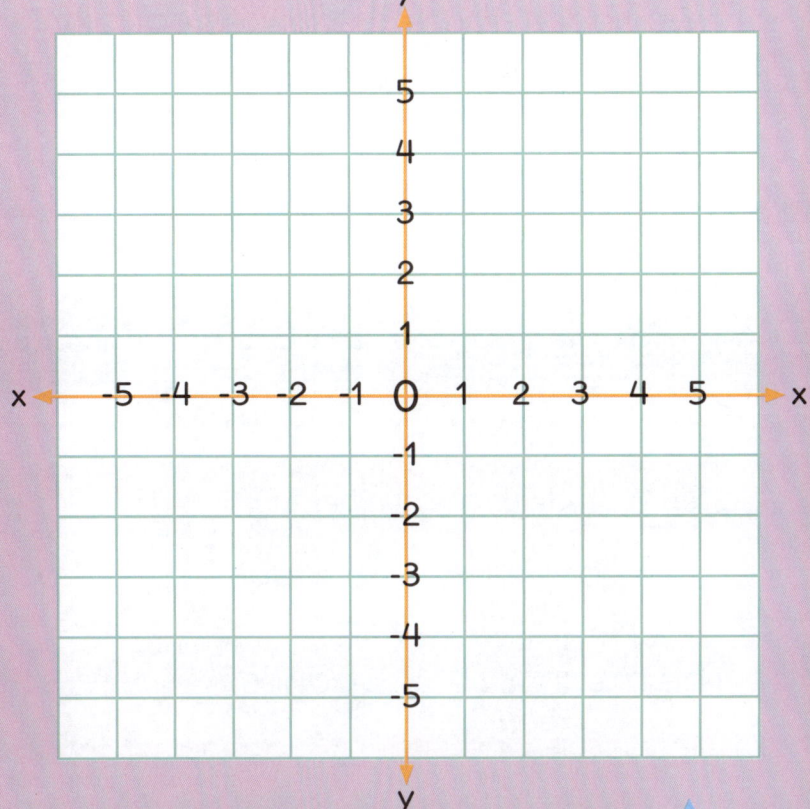

Finding the Mean

The **mean** in a data set is often called the average. In the data below, the mean is the number of bones each dog would have if they were distributed equally.

Charlie has 4 bones, Otto has 3, Buster 6, Rex 3, Enzo 4, Scout 5, and Rolo 3.

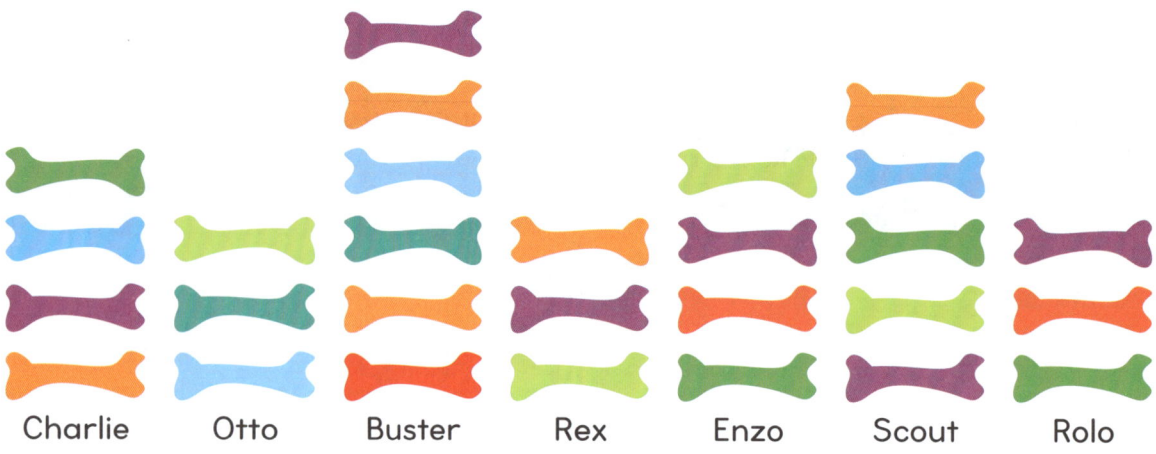

If we redistribute the bones equally they would each have 4 bones.

We can calculate the mean in 2 steps:

Step 1: Find the total number of bones.

4 + 3 + 6 + 3 + 4 + 5 + 3 = ☐ bones

Step 2: Divide by the number of dogs.

☐ bones ÷ ☐ dogs = ☐ bones

The mean is ☐ bones.

Note for student: You need to be familiar with the math vocabulary used in statistics.

Now try these:

1. Calculate the mean number of points scored by the football teams in the data below:

Name	Points Scored
Sharks	25
Tigers	30
Ravens	35
Bears	23
Vipers	28
Wolves	27

Step 1: Find the total number of points.

25 + 30 + 35 + 23 + 28 + 27 = ☐

Step 2: Divide by the number of teams.

☐ ÷ 6 = ☐

Mean number of points scored: ☐

2. Calculate the mean rainfall over a week in Raineetown.

Day	Rainfall in inches (in.)
Monday	5.13
Tuesday	4.56
Wednesday	6.71
Thursday	4.25
Friday	5.80
Saturday	0.00
Sunday	5.75

Step 1: Find the total rainfall for the week.

Total rainfall = ☐ in.

You can use a calculator if you wish.

Step 2: Divide by the number of days.

☐ ÷ ☐ = ☐ in.

Mean rainfall in Raineetown over the week: ☐ in.

Refer back to the data table above to answer these questions.

a. Which days had more rainfall than the mean? ....

b. Which days had less rainfall than the mean? ....

c. Calculate the difference in inches between the driest and the wettest day.

The range is ☐ in.

d. What is unusual about the data for Saturday? ....

Finding the Median

The median is the middle value in a set of data.
To figure out the median:

Step 1: Write the values in order.   **Step 2:** Find the middle value.

Example: Figure out the median weight of these 8 suitcases.

From the lightest to the heaviest, the suitcases weigh:

~~18 lb.,~~ ~~20 lb.,~~ ~~21 lb.,~~ (22 lb., 23 lb.,) ~~24 lb.,~~ ~~25 lb.,~~ ~~27 lb.~~

The middle value is between 22 and 23 lb., so the median is $22\frac{1}{2}$ lb.

1. Find the median height of these 5 buildings.

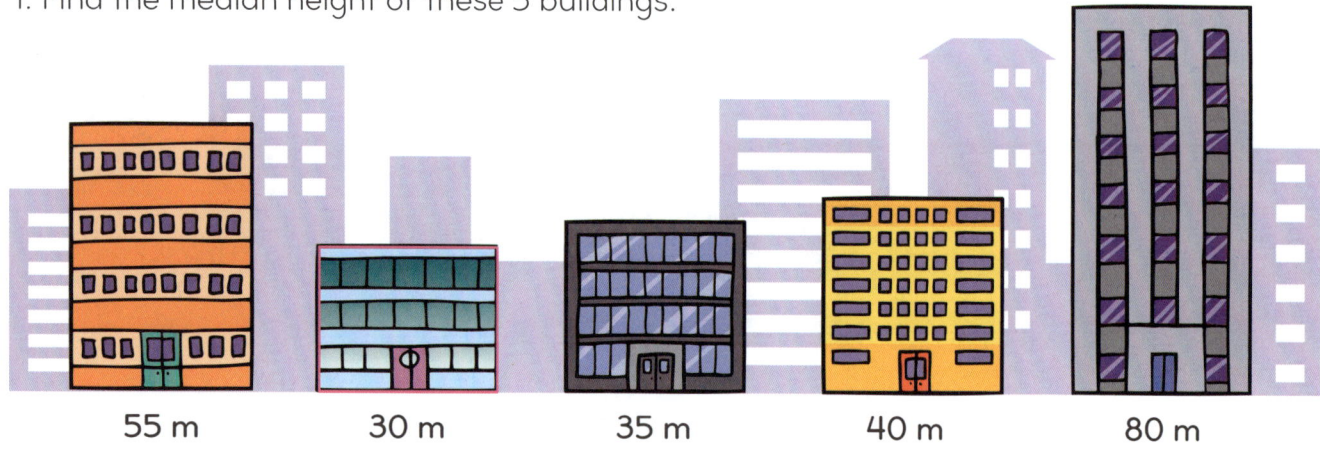

55 m   30 m   35 m   40 m   80 m

Step 1. Write the heights in order of size:

....

Step 2. Find the middle value.   The median is  m.

Note for student: It is important to remember how mean and median are different, and involve different calculations.

Mean, Median, and Range

The table below shows the weights of 5 football players in the college team. Answer the following questions based on the data.

Player 1	Player 2	Player 3	Player 4	Player 5
195 lb.	230 lb.	213 lb.	205 lb.	252 lb.

1. What is the mean or average weight of the players in the team?

195 + ☐ + ☐ + ☐ + ☐ = ☐ lb.

☐ ÷ ☐ = ☐ lb.   The mean weight is ☐ lb.

2. What is the range in weight of the players in the team?

☐ lb. − ☐ lb. = ☐ lb.

The range is ☐ lb.

3. What is the median weight of the players?

☐ ☐ ☐ ☐ ☐

The median weight is ☐ lb.

4. If player 1 is substituted by a player weighing 200 lb., how would your calculations change? Circle the correct answers.

The mean would be: greater / smaller / the same

The range would be: greater / smaller / the same

The median would be: greater / smaller / the same

Note for student: You need to be know about the different ways in which data can be analyzed and described.

More Mean Data Problems

See below the prices of the birthday cakes in four different stores.

As a super math challenge, you could try to calculate your answers mentally! Give it a try!

Bob's Bakehouse $5

Colette's Confectionary $7

Pablo's Pasteleria $10

Priti's Patisserie $12

1. What is the average price of a birthday cake at these stores?

Average price: ☐ ÷ ☐ = $ ☐

2. By how much is Colette's price below the average price? $ ☐

3. By how much is Priti's price above the average price? $ ☐

4. What is the range in the prices of birthday cakes across the stores? $ ☐

5. If a fifth store opened selling birthday cakes for $6, would the average price go up or down, and by how much? Circle the correct answer.

The average price would   go up / down   by $ ☐

Note for student: Using math to make price comparisons is a handy skill that could save you money!

Answers

Language Arts and Reading

Page 6
The ball went to the left of the goal posts.
The highway is beside the river.
The restaurant was on the opposite side of the road.
There was a fence between the two houses.
"If we go to the right we should arrive at the beach."

Page 7
dance: had danced, have danced, will have danced.
drive: had driven, have driven, will have driven.
clean: had cleaned, have cleaned, will have cleaned.
play: had played, have played, will have played.
sleep: had slept, have slept, will have slept.
swim: had swum, have swum, will have swum.
sing: had sung, have sung, will have sung.

Page 8
Possible answers in the order they appear in the letter:
However, In addition, Moreover, Therefore, Consequently, For example.

Page 9
Possible answers include:
1. whether/or, 2. either/or,
3. both/and, 4. not only/but also,
5. neither/nor, 6. whether/or,
7. either/or, 8. neither/nor.

Page 10
Trolls may be intimidating, ugly, and foul-smelling adversaries, but do not despair. Follow this handy guide to help rid yourself of these troublesome, mischievous pests. You will need: a large lump of meat, some air freshener, a nose plug, and a drum or other loud instrument. The bridges, where trolls like to make their dens, are found over fast-flowing rivers. Place your meat nearby. While staying hidden, make a lot of noise to draw the troll's attention. Trolls are always hungry, so they won't be able to resist a tasty treat. While the troll is enjoying its feast, sneak under the bridge to find its den. While wearing your nose plug, because a troll den is stinky, spray your air freshener. Trolls hate nice smelling things, so when your troll returns home you can be sure they won't be sticking around!

Page 11
After overcoming many trials, Sinbad and his crew finally spied the ruins of an ancient city looming above the treetops.
"I was right, wasn't I?" grinned Sinbad. "We made it to the city."
"Yes, but I don't see any gold," said Shireen. "You promised my father riches beyond his wildest dreams."
"You must have faith, Shireen," laughed Sinbad. "Have I ever let you down?"
Shireen put a finger to her chin thoughtfully. "Yes, that time when I got captured by giants. Don't you remember, Sinbad?"
"That's true, I agree," he shrugged. "However, I did come to your rescue."
"No, actually I freed myself. And the time when I was stuck in that swamp."
"You have a good memory, Shireen," smirked Sinbad. "This time will be different."
Shireen rolled her eyes. "Let's see, Sinbad. Lead the way."

Pages 12–13
Possible answers include:
1. The pilot of the supersonic jet liked to show off his skills.
2. The pirate with the scowl on his face threatened to take the gold.
3. Cinderella was very excited to be going to the ball.
4. The rookie team finally won the Champions League.
5. The cruise ship was going to hit the iceberg!

Possible answers include:
2. I play the piano, but my brother plays the guitar. (run on)
3. The car keys were missing from the drawer. (fragment)
4. The bag was heavy because I packed too much. (run on)
5. The cat was frightened because she heard a loud bang. (fragment)

Page 14
scrawny (remarkable) smirk lazy confused
(generous) (dedicated) argument smug cheap
(creative) impulsive stressed demanded stench
1. smirk, 2. argument, 3. demanded, 4. confused, 5. smug, 6. stench, 7. lazy, 8. scrawny.

Page 15
Possible answers include:
1. Formal, 2. Formal, 3. Informal, 4. Informal, 5. Formal.
As a formal article, you could write something like this: On Friday, March 20th, the children in sixth grade took part in "The Book Run" to raise funds for a new school library. The challenge was to complete four laps of the school fields. Despite the rain and the mud, everyone managed to successfully complete the run. Well done, sixth graders!

Pages 18–19
Possible answers include:
1. The innkeeper's son. He writes that his father runs the Admiral Benbow Inn.
2. The Old Sea-Dog is the old skipper who calls himself the captain.
3. berth (6), connoisseur (8), grog-shop (1), more was the pity (2), mought (7), sittyated (3), skipper (5), threshold (4).
4. The scar is described as a sabre cut of a dirty, livid white.
5. accustomed to—used to; whole particulars—every detail; trundled—pushed.
6. (He is hiding) He is pleased that the inn does not have many customers and he chose it because it was described as lonely.

123

Pages 18–19 cont.
(He is looking for someone) He chose the inn because it is near the coast and has a good view of the ships coming in and out of the port.

Pages 22–23
Possible answers include:
1. Sky Father is hiding all the light from in the world inside the box.
2. We know his daughter is unhappy because she cries every day.
3. Raven becomes a child and begs for a toy to play with.
4. Raven is right to steal the light because the world is in darkness and he is always bumping into things. Sky Father's daughter is also sad because she cannot find a husband.
5. The narrator is sympathetic toward Raven because the text says, "He would often find himself flying into trees and rocks." Sky Father is described as "miserly" and wants to keep the light for himself.
6. We learn that Sky Father is lonely because he has lost his wife and does not want his daughter to leave him. He made the light so he has the right to keep it.

Pages 26–27
bald eagle differences:
340° vision   good at distance
three eyelids   two focal points
dragonfly differences:
360° vision   nearsighted
large compound eyes
bald eagle and dragonfly both have:
fixed eyes   can see ultraviolet light

1. Both the bald eagle and the chameleon…
2. Unlike the bald eagle and the dragonfly, the eyes of the chameleon…
3. Humans have a single focal point…
4. In contrast to the eyes of the bald eagle, those of the dragonfly…
lion (predator),   zebra (prey),
jack rabbit (prey), deer (prey),
coyote (predator), red fox (predator).

Pages 28–29
Possible answers include:
1. Louis Braille became blind after an accident in his father's workshop. He scratched one eye, which then became infected. The infection spread to his other eye, leaving him blind by the age of five.
2. Louis was dissatisfied with the books at the institute because they were large and heavy, and would take a long time to read.
3. Barbier's system was useful for soldiers because they could send messages to each other without alerting the enemy.
4. Louis improved the Barbier system by reducing the number of dots. He also included all the letters of the alphabet, as well as numbers and punctuation marks.
5. Students at the institute found Braille's system easier to learn and quicker to read. They could also use the system to take notes in class.
6. Louis was twenty years old when he published his first book in Braille.
7. Following Louis Braille's death, his system became the standard reading method for the blind in France, and was eventually made the official reading system for all blind people around the world.

Pages 30–31
Possible answers include:
1. seizeth—to take hold of something
range—to search an area
procure—to achieve a goal
2. The poet admires the slow, quiet, and calm nature of the snail.
3. The poet is teaching us that success is achieved by taking your time and making steady progress rather than being hasty and careless.

1. Snail is quiet and calm, and more patient than the other animals. She does not give up on her plan.
2. Yes, the poets share similar viewpoints because in both texts, the snail achieves success by being patient and hardworking, and not giving in to brashness or hastiness.

Pages 32–33
Possible answers include:
gyre—to whirl or spin
shun—to ignore or avoid
foe—an enemy
burbled—to make a bubbling sound
galumphing—to move in a noisy and clumsy way
chortled—to laugh joyously
1. "Slithy toves did gyre" might refer to a type of slimy creature that is gyrating or moving around in circles. Many made-up creatures feature in the poem, such as borogroves and mome raths.
2. starving + ravenous = starvenous
massive + enormous = massormous
dreadful + horrible = dreadible
3. He may be frustrated that he hasn't found the Jabberwocky and is wondering what to do next.
4. uffish thought: grumpy
came whiffling: creeping
tulgey wood: dense wood
5. The son slays the Jabberwocky by cutting off its head. He returns home to his father, who hugs him with joy.
6. Oh, what a wonderful day! Hurrah! Hooray!

Pages 34–35
1. The author believes that everyone should introduce exercise into their lives.
2. The author has written the article to challenge the negative views that some children have about exercise.
3. Physical health: Exercise is good for the heart and lungs, and can reduce the risk of illnesses, such as diabetes.
Brain health: A study has shown that exercise can help improve the brain area responsible for memory and learning.
Self-esteem: Setting exercise goals can provide a sense of accomplishment and help with self-confidence.
4. Some children think that exercise is boring. The author answers this by suggesting that children choose an activity that is exciting and fun, and will keep them motivated.

Writing

Page 38
Topic sentence: Saturn is known as the ringed planet.

Detail one: It is surrounded by rings of rock and ice.
Detail two: They can be seen from Earth with a telescope.
Concluding sentence: The rings make Saturn a fascinating planet.

Page 39
When it's too dark to see, we simply flick a switch. <u>However</u>, the invention of the light bulb took many years to perfect. <u>First</u>, English scientist Humphrey Davy invented the arc lamp. <u>Although</u> the invention worked, it was far too large and dangerous to be used in the home. <u>Therefore</u>, inventors had to come up with a better idea. <u>Finally</u>, around 1850, two scientists, Thomas Edison and Joseph Swan, <u>simultaneously</u> developed a safe working light bulb. <u>Initially</u>, they argued over who had invented it first, but <u>eventually</u> they settled their differences and worked together. <u>Thus,</u> they were able to refine their designs and bring light to the world!

Page 40
Possible headings include:
Title: Cat's Eyes—A Clever Invention
Subheading: A cat to the rescue!
Subheading: Time for reflection
Subheading: Lighting the world's roads
Caption: How a real cat's eye works

Page 41
Main idea: B.
Supporting details: A. D. E.
tapetum lucidum: a layer of cells behind the retina that reflect light.
patent: a document that protects an inventor's idea.
Best quotation: Alan Whicker, journalist.

Pages 44–45
1895: William Tappendon sets up the world's first potato chip factory.
1926: Laura Scudder invents the potato chip bag.
1954: Joe Murphy develops different flavors of potato chip.

Page 50
1. personification, 2. alliteration, 3. oxymoron.

Page 51
Possible answers include:
Best describe the Moon—like a watchful eye, like a shiny pearl, as pale as winter.
Best describe a calm sea—a blue blanket, a glittering treasure, a polished mirror.

Pages 52–53
Possible answers include:
1. The sun is being compared to the captain of a ship.
2. The poet is describing the cycle of day and night.
3. The poem is likely to be set in ancient times because the captain is using a lodestone to navigate, and his ship uses oars instead of an engine. He is also wearing linen, a common fabric in the ancient world.
4. When night falls, the ship sails through a dark gloomy land of ghosts and monsters.
5. Personification helps us to picture the movement of the sun in an exciting and engaging way. We feel as though we are on an adventure with the captain of the ship.

Pages 56–57
2. Rising action—Raven puts his plan into action to steal the light.
3. Climax—Raven steals the light from the box.
4. Falling action—Raven loses the light as a result of a chase.
5. Resolution—Light is restored to the world, and the daughter marries.

Page 58
I wrestled with the controls of my spacecraft. Alarm bells were ringing and warning lights flashing. I knew that things were going from bad to worse. The engine was losing power and soon my thrusters would cease to work. Behind me, the alien mothership was closing in. I turned my ship into a steep dive toward the nearby asteroids. I was the best pilot in the academy but was I good enough to make it through alive? I told myself, I can do it!

Decimals and Fractions

Page 65
$10^2 = 100$
$10^3 = 1,000$
$10^4 = 1,000 \times 10 = 10,000$
$10^5 = 10,000 \times 10 = 100,000$
$10^6 = 100,000 \times 10 = 1,000,000$
3 zeros, 4 zeros, 5 zeros, 6 zeros
$10^7 = 10 \times 10 \times 10 \times 10 \times 10 \times 10 \times 10 = 10,000,000$
$10^8 = 10 \times 10 \times 10 \times 10 \times 10 \times 10 \times 10 \times 10 = 100,000,000$
$10^9 = 10 \times 10 \times 10 \times 10 \times 10 \times 10 \times 10 \times 10 \times 10 = 1,000,000,000$
$10^{10} = 10 \times 10 \times 10 \times 10 \times 10 \times 10 \times 10 \times 10 \times 10 \times 10 = 10,000,000,000$

Pages 66–67
$22 \times 2 = 44$
$22 \times 10 = 220$
$22 \times 20 = 440$
Each child gets 22 stickers.

This problem could be written as $630 \div 15$.
$15 \times 2 = 30$
$15 \times 10 = 150$
$15 \times 20 = 300$
$15 \times 40 = 600$

42 minibuses will be needed.

This problem could be written as $552 \div 24$.
$24 \times 2 = 48$
$24 \times 10 = 240$
$24 \times 20 = 480$

There are 23 rows of people.

Page 68
1. 23
2. 5
3. 175
4. 560
5. 180
6. 4,215

Page 69
1. 0.99
2. 1.73
3. 4.86
4. 3.84
5. 0.52
6. 4.99

Pages 70-71

8.96 × 4 =
```
    3 2
    8 . 9 6
  ×       4
  3 5 . 8 4
```
Product = 35.84

1.01 × 0.5 =
```
    1 . 0 1
  ×     0 . 5
      5 0 5
    0 0 0 0
    0 . 5 0 5
```
Product = 0.505

6.95 × 5.1 =
```
        4 2
      6 . 9 5
  ×       5 . 1
      6 9 5
  3 4 7 5 0
  3 5 . 4 4 5
```
Product = 35.445

17.45 × 3.2 =
```
      2 1 1 1
      1 7 . 4 5
  ×         3 . 2
      3 4 9 0
  5 2 3 5 0
  5 5 . 8 4 0
```
Product = 55.840

Pages 72-73
36.6 ÷ 6 =   6.1   6)36.6
28.44 ÷ 4 =   7.11   4)28.44
837.6 ÷ 2 =   418.8   2)837.6
98.8 ÷ 0.4 =   247   4)988.
25.5 ÷ 0.5 =   51   5)255.

Pages 74-75
$\frac{36}{3}$ = 12 They each earn 12 dollars.

1. $\frac{24}{6}$ = 4 party favors in each bag.
2. $\frac{64}{8}$ = 8 bulbs in each pot.
3. They each have to write $\frac{19}{2}$ = $9\frac{1}{2}$ pages.
4. They each get $\frac{28}{8}$ = $3\frac{4}{8}$ = $3\frac{1}{2}$ sheets.

Pages 76-77
1. $\frac{4}{1} \times \frac{3}{5} = \frac{12}{5} = 2\frac{2}{5}$
2. $\frac{5}{1} \times \frac{5}{6} = \frac{25}{6} = 4\frac{1}{6}$
3. $\frac{3}{1} \times \frac{3}{4} = \frac{9}{4} = 2\frac{1}{4}$
4. $\frac{6}{1} \times \frac{5}{8} = \frac{30}{8} = 3\frac{6}{8} = 3\frac{3}{4}$
5. $\frac{7}{1} \times \frac{3}{10} = \frac{21}{10} = 2\frac{1}{10}$
6. $\frac{8}{1} \times \frac{7}{8} = \frac{56}{8} = 7$
7. $\frac{9}{1} \times \frac{5}{12} = \frac{45}{12} = 3\frac{9}{12} = 3\frac{3}{4}$

Pages 78-79
1. $\frac{1}{12}$
2. $\frac{1}{8}$
3. $\frac{2}{12} = \frac{1}{6}$
4. $\frac{3}{10}$

Pages 80-81
1. $\frac{4}{5} \times \frac{3}{4} = \frac{12}{20} = \frac{3}{5}$ Area = $\frac{3}{5}$ square units
Parts that overlap → $\frac{12}{20} = \frac{3}{5}$
Total number of parts

2. $\frac{5}{6} \times \frac{1}{2} = \frac{5}{12}$ Area = $\frac{5}{12}$ square units
Parts that overlap → $\frac{5}{12}$
Total number of parts

Pages 82-83
1. Each child gets $\frac{1}{12}$ of the whole sheet of stickers.
$\frac{1}{12} \times 4 = \frac{1}{3}$

2. $\frac{1}{2} \div 3 = \frac{1}{6}$
Each child gets $\frac{1}{6}$ of the pencils in the box. $\frac{1}{6} \times 3 = \frac{1}{2}$

3. $\frac{1}{4} \div 2 = \frac{1}{8}$
We each get $\frac{1}{8}$ of the whole pizza.
$\frac{1}{8} \times 2 = \frac{1}{4}$

4. $\frac{1}{3} \div 3 = \frac{1}{9}$
Each dog gets $\frac{1}{9}$ of all the biscuits in the box. $\frac{1}{9} \times 3 = \frac{1}{3}$

Pages 84-85
1. $20 \times \frac{1}{5} = 4$
2. $3 \div \frac{1}{8} = 24$ $24 \times \frac{1}{8} = 3$
3. $3 \div \frac{1}{6} = 18$ $18 \times \frac{1}{6} = 3$
4. $4 \div \frac{1}{4} = 16$ $16 \times \frac{1}{4} = 4$

Page 86
1. 4 flowers to 8 bees = 4 : 8
2. 6 chocolate cookies to 4 cupcakes = 6 : 4
3. 7 pentagons to 5 triangles = 7 : 5
4. 10 blue pens to 5 red pens = 10 : 5

Page 87
4 cookies

Milkshakes	1	2	3	4	7	10	15	22
Cookies	2	4	6	8	14	20	30	44

1. 10 milkshakes
2. 14 cookies
3. 30 cookies
4. 22 milkshakes

Page 88
1. 5 oranges sold : 1 apple sold

Oranges	5	50
Apples	1	10

50 oranges sold : 10 apples sold

2.
Oranges	8	32
Liters of juice	1	4

8 oranges : 1 liter
32 oranges : 4 liters

3.
Cups of flour	5	15
Cups of water	2	6

5 cups of flour : 2 cups of water
15 cups of flour : 6 cups of water

Page 89
9 : 12 has the same ratio as 3 : 4

Bue cans	3	9	12	15
Yellow cans	4	12	16	20

Four equivalent ratios = 8:2, 16:4, 4:1, 80:20.

Pages 90-91

1. 70 ÷ 5 = 14 pages per day
She writes at a rate of 14 pages per day.
To write 56 pages, it will take 56 ÷ 14 = 4 days.
To write her book, it will take 168 ÷ 14 = 12 days.

2. 15 ÷ 6 = 2.5 miles per hour
He runs at a rate of 2.5 miles per hour.
15 ÷ 3 = 5 hours
Jamal ran the race in 5 hours.

3. 800 mi ÷ 500 mi/h = time
8 ÷ 5 = 1.6 hours
0.6 of 60 minutes = 36 minutes
Or,
$\frac{8}{5} = 1\frac{3}{5}$ hours
To find minutes: $\frac{3}{5}$ of 60 minutes = 36 minutes
1 hour 36 minutes

Pages 92-93

50% of 24 = 12 pencils
$\frac{50}{100} \times 24$ Simplify: $\frac{1}{2} \times \frac{24}{1} = \frac{24}{2} = 12$
Jackson gave his sister 12 pencils.

1. $\frac{60}{100} \times \frac{15}{1}$
Simplify: $\frac{3}{5} \times \frac{15}{1} = \frac{45}{5} = 9$
They won 9 games.

2. $\frac{25}{100} \times \frac{48}{1}$
Simplify: $\frac{1}{4} \times \frac{48}{1} = \frac{48}{4} = 12$
The discount was $12
After discount, the coat cost $36.

3. $\frac{30}{100} \times \frac{70}{1}$
Simplify: $\frac{3}{10} \times \frac{70}{1} = \frac{210}{10} = 21$
He sold 21 chocolate cookies.

Measurement, Data, and Geometry

Page 96

1. 72 in.
2. 4 ft.
3. 5 ft., 60 ÷ 12 = 5
4. 120 in., 10 × 12 = 120
5. 45 ft., 15 × 3 = 45
6. 33 yd., 99 ÷ 3 = 33

Page 97

1. 600 cm   2. 165 mm
3. 600 m   4. 6 km

Page 98

1. 1 lb. 4 oz.   2. 192 oz.
3. 800 oz., 50 × 16 = 800
4. 6 lb., 96 ÷ 16 = 6
5. 12,000 lb., 6 × 2,000 = 12,000
6. 4 tn., 8,000 ÷ 2,000 = 4
7. 14 lb., 224 ÷ 16 = 14
8. 50,000 lb., 25 × 2,000 = 50,000

Page 99

1. 5 kg   2. 7,000 g
3. 6,000 g   4. 4 kg
5. 5,500 g   6. 3.5 kg

Page 100

1. 24 pt.   2. 12 c.   3. 40 qt.
4. 4 pt.   5. 2 gal. 6. 4 gal.

Page 101

Quantity in mL	Quantity in L	As a Fraction
100 mL	0.10 L	$\frac{1}{10}$ L
200 mL	0.20 L	$\frac{2}{10}$ or $\frac{1}{5}$ L
300 mL	0.30 L	$\frac{3}{10}$ L
400 mL	0.40 L	$\frac{4}{10}$ or $\frac{2}{5}$ L
800 mL	0.80 L	$\frac{8}{10}$ or $\frac{4}{5}$ L
1,100 mL	1.10 L	$1\frac{1}{10}$ L

Pages 102-103

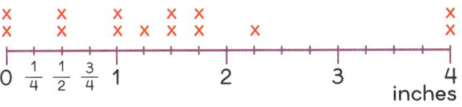

1. 4 in.   2. 2 days
3. 3 days   4. 21 in.
7 + 6 + 8 = 21

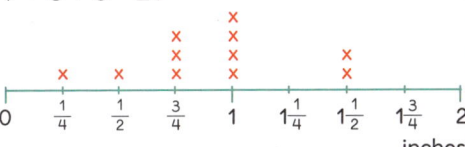

1. $1\frac{1}{2}$ in.   2. $\frac{1}{4}$ in.   3. $1\frac{1}{4}$ in.
4. 10 in. $\frac{3}{4} + 2\frac{1}{4} + 4 + 3 = 10$
5. 5 in.

Page 104

1. True
2. False
3. False
4. True

1. A parallelogram has 2 pairs of parallel sides.
2. A square has 4 sides the same length and 4 right angles.

Page 105

Shapes with 2 pairs of parallel sides: parallelogram, square, rhombus, rectangle.
Shapes with all sides the same length: square, regular hexagon, rhombus, equilateral triangle.
Shapes with 4 right angles: rectangle, square.

Pages 106-107

Shape A: Volume = 9 + 9 + 9 = 27 cubic units.
Shape B: Volume = 8 × 2 = 16 cubic units.

1. V = 20 × 10 × 20 = 4,000 cubic inches.
2. V = 5 × 5 × 15 = 375 cubic centimeters.
3. V = 20 × 8 × 8 = 1,280 cubic feet.

Pages 108–109
1. A = 4 × 3 × 4 = 48 cm³
   B = 8 × 3 × 4 = 96 cm³
Total volume = A + B = 144 cm³
2. A = 4 × 3 × 5 = 60 m³
   B = 12 × 3 × 6 = 216 m³
Total volume = A + B = 276 m³

1. Crayons = 10 × 3 × 4 = 120 in.³
   Pencils = 3 × 3 × 8 = 72 in.³
Total volume = 120 + 72 = 192 in.³
2. Closet = 4 × 2 × 7 = 56 ft.³
   Cupboard = 3 × 2 × 5 = 30 ft.³
Total volume = 56 + 30 = 86 ft.³

Pages 110–111
Pirate ship = (1,5)
Crocodile swamp = (2,2)
Scorpion Island = (6,1)

Start at (2,1), walk one square North East to reach (3,2). Look out for crocodiles! Walk one square North to the footbridge at (3,3), then continue North three squares to reach Skull Rock at (3,6). Walk one square East to (4,6), then walk one square South East to dig for the treasure at (5,5)! Now make your way back. Walk two squares South to the tall palm tree at (5,3). The river is shallow enough to cross. Continue one square South West to (4,2) then walk one square South to (4,1). Walk two squares West to reach (2,1), back where you started from.

2. 3 miles South.   3. 2 miles East.
4. 4 miles West.

Pages 112–113
1. -5, -3, 3, 6   -30, 0, 20, 50
2. -2.2, 3.5, -5.4, -1.9, -6.6, -4.1
3. a. 24°F > -24°F
   b. -80°F > -88°F
   c. -56°F < -50°F

4. Nisha has the most money.
5. a. $-5 > $-8   b. $-4 < $4
   c. $-10 < $1   d. $15 > $-20
   e. $-7 < $70   f. $50 > $-25

Pages 114
A. 70°F B. 52°F C. 10°F D. -10°F
The coldest city is Ottawa.
The warmest city is Singapore.
The difference in temperature between the coldest and the warmest city is 53°F.

Pages 115
1. The nighttime temperature will be -12°C.
2. The temperature will be -19°C.
3. He will have $-8 in his bank account.
4. She will have $-6 in her bank account.

Pages 116–117
1.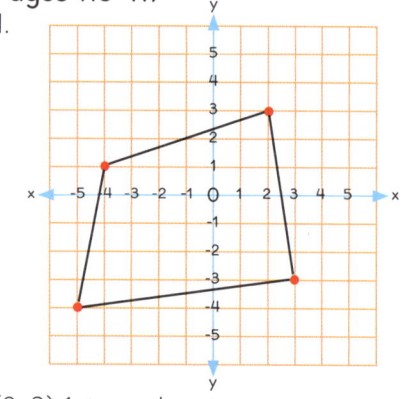
(2, 3) 1st quadrant
(-4, 1) 2nd quadrant
(-5, -4) 3rd quadrant
(3, -3) 4th quadrant

2.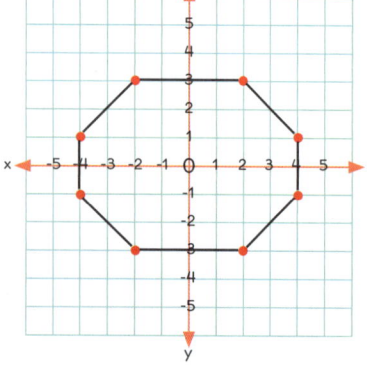
You should have made an octagon.

Pages 118–119
Step 1: 28 bones
Step 2: 28 bones ÷ 7 dogs = 4 bones
The mean is 4 bones.

1. Step 1: 168 points
Step 2: 168 ÷ 6 = 28
Mean number of points scored: 28
2. Step 1: Total rainfall = 32.2 in.
Step 2: 32.2 ÷ 7 = 4.6 in.
Mean rainfall in Raineetown over the week = 4.6 in.
a. Monday, Wednesday, Friday, and Sunday
b. Tuesday, Thursday and Saturday
c. The range is 6.71 in.
4. There is no data for Saturday, which is unusual.

Page 120
Step 1: 30 m, 35 m, 40 m, 55 m, 80 m
Step 2: The median is 40 m

Page 121
1. 195 + 230 + 213 + 205 + 252 = 1,095 lb.
1,095 ÷ 5 = 219 lb.
The mean weight is 219 lb.
2. 252 lb. – 195 lb. = 57 lb.
The range is 57 lb.
3. 195, 205, 213, 230, 252
The median weight is 213 lb.

4. The mean would be: greater
The range would be: smaller
The median would be: the same

Page 122
1. Average price: $34 ÷ 4 = $8.50
2. $1.50
3. $3.50
4. $7
5. The average price would go down by $0.50 because $40 ÷ 5 = $8